Justice Under Siege

One Woman's Battle Against
a European Oil Company

Eva Joly

Justice Under Siege

One Woman's Battle Against a European Oil Company

Translated from the French by Emma Kemp

ARCADIA BOOKS
CITIZEN PRESS
LONDON 2006

Arcadia Books Ltd
15-16 Nassau Street
London W1W 7AB
www.arcadiabooks.co.uk
and
Citizen Press

First published in the United Kingdom 2006
Originally published by Editions des Arènes 2003
Copyright © Editions des Arènes 2003

This English translation from the French,
Est-ce dans ce monde-là que nous voulons vivre?
Copyright © Emma Kemp 2006

ISBN 1905147465

Typeset in Bembo by Basement Press
Printed in Finland by WS Bookwell

Arcadia Books supports English PEN, the fellowship of writers who work together to promote
literature and its understanding. English PEN upholds writers' freedoms in Britain and around
the world, challenging political and cultural limits on free expression. To find out more, visit
www.englishpen.org or contact
English PEN, 6-8 Amwell Street, London EC1R 1UQ

Arcadia Books distributors are as follows:

in the UK and elsewhere in Europe:
Turnaround Publishers Services
Unit 3, Olympia Trading Estate
Coburg Road
London N22 6TZ

in the US and Canada:
Independent Publishers Group
814 N. Franklin Street
Chicago, IL 60610

in Australia:
Tower Books
PO Box 213 Brookvale, NSW 2100

in New Zealand:
Addenda
PO Box 78224
Grey Lynn Auckland

in South Africa:
Quartet Sales and Marketing
PO Box 1218
Northcliffe
Johannesburg 2115

Arcadia Books is the *Sunday Times* Small Publisher of the Year

Acknowledgements

In Norway, thanks to Helle and Anniken, Guro, Jens-Petter, Rolf-Einar, Per-Ludvig, Bjørg, Jørn, Olav, Sonja, Marit, Kari, Tone, Anne-Mette, Katherine, Atle, Jan and Unn.

In France, thanks to Patricia, Tanja, Julien, Caroloine, Thomas, Dominique, Christian, Pierre, Serge, Jacques, Vincent, Emmanuel, Laurence, Elisabeth, Jean-Baptiste and Sophie.

In the United States, thanks to David, Kristina, Lucy and Enery.

In Italy, thanks to Leo.

In Mexico, thanks to Raoul.

In the Philippines, thanks to Jak.

In Switzerland, thanks to Bernard, Paul, Curtil, Sylvie and Gretta.

In India, thanks to Anita, Arne and Mahendra.

In Canada, thanks to Louise.

In the United Kingdom, thanks to Lucinda and Michel.

At the moment we're only living in the time of the cops. The real time for the judges will come tomorrow, whether you like it or not; and it will be that of the just judges.
Marc Bloch

I don't have any justification to back up the confidence I have in the future of mankind. It's possible that it's not rational. But despair is irrational: it doesn't resolve any problems, it even creates new ones and is by its very nature an affliction. It's true that some of my stories end in catastrophe; but if we raise our defences in time, we have the means, the intelligence and the strength to overcome it.
Primo Levi

This book is dedicated to all those who have paid with their lives for their refusal to give way to corruption, to the journalists and judges who died just doing their job, in particular:

François Renaud, investigating magistrate in Lyons, assassinated on 3rd July 1975.

Don Bolles, journalist with the *Arizona Republic*, killed when his car was blown up in the United States on 2nd June 1976. He was investigating the secret links between industry, the political world and organised crime.

Pierre Michel, investigating magistrate in Marseilles, assassinated on 21st October 1981.

Hernando Baquero Borda, Colombian Supreme Court judge, assassinated on 31st July 1986.

Antonino Saette, presiding judge in the appeal court of Palermo, Sicily, assassinated on 26th September 1988, with his son Stefano.

Ivan Martinez Vela, president of the High Court of Ecuador, cut down by three bullets on the 24th October 1988.

Giovanni Falcone, anti-mafia public prosecutor in Palermo, assassinated with his wife and three bodyguards on 23rd May 1992.

Paolo Borsellino, anti-Mafia public prosecutor in Palermo, assassinated with five members of his escort on 19th July 1992.

Veronica Guerin, journalist specialising in criminal matters for the Sunday Independent, shot in Ireland on 26th June 1996. She had written numerous articles on the criminal underworld and the flourishing drugs trade in Ireland.

Norbert Zongo, director of the newspaper *L'Indépendant*, assassinated in Burkina Faso on 13th December 1998. He had revealed several financial scandals compromising those close to President Blaise Compaoré.

Hector Jiménez Rodriguez, civil court judge in Medellin, Colombia, assassinated 17th October 1999.

Carlos Cardoso, Mozambican investigative journalist, assassinated in November 2000. For several years he had exposed corruption at the highest level of politics and the judiciary, and was investigating an affair which implicated the Commercial Bank of Mozambique when he was killed.

Gueorgui Gongadze, journalist and creator of an internet site dedicated to the exposure of the Ukrainian authorities, kidnapped in September 2000. His decapitated body was discovered two months later.

Feng Zhaoxia, journalist with the Chinese daily Gejie Daobao, found dead with his throat cut on the 15th January 2001. In his articles he had exposed connivance between mafia groups and local political figures.

Gueorgui Sanaïa, journalist for the independent Georgian TV channel Rustai 2, shot in the head on the 26th July 2001. The daily programme which he presented was famous for making accusations of corruption and racketeering against the public prosecutor's department and the Minister for National Security.

Jorge Mynor Alegría Armendáriz, journalist with Radio Amatique in Guatemala, assassinated outside his home by persons unknown, on 5th September 2001. He had exposed corruption within the authorities.

Paul Nkoué, Cameroon magistrate, assassinated on 17th February 2002.

Harun-al-Rashid, journalist for the daily newspaper *Dainik Purbanchal*, assassinated in Bangladesh on 2nd March 2002. He had written articles on organised crime in the south-west of the country, and in particular on the mafia tendencies of the Purba Bangla Sharbahara Party.

Valeri Ivanov, editor of the newspaper of the *Russian city, Togliatti*, assassinated in May 2002. He had just written a series of reports on corruption amongst local officials.

Edgar Damalerio, reporter for Radio DXKP and director of the Zamboanga Scribe, shot in the Philippines on the 13th May 2002. He had published numerous articles on corruption amongst politicians and the police.

Leïla Baisetova, kidnapped, tortured and assassinated in Kazakhstan on 23rd May 2002. The previous day, her mother, the journalist Lira Baisetova, had published an interview with Prosecutor Bernard Bertossa which revealed the existence of Swiss bank accounts in the names of two former Kazakh prime ministers. Lira Baisetova, who had been threatened for months, had already lost an eye after a previous assault.

Sonny Alcantara, publisher of the Filipino newspaper *Kokus* and television journalist, killed by a shot to the head on the 22nd August 2002. He knew he was at risk because of his articles written in opposition to the previous mayor of San Pablo City.

Hector Rodriguez, magistrate with the administrative court of Guatemala City, assassinated on the 12th January 2003.

Guillermo Bravo and **Jaime Rengifo**, television journalist and radio reporter respectively, assassinated on the 28th and 29th April 2003 in Colombia. Both had uncovered corruption scandals and exposed the activities of armed groups.

Contents

The Elf Affair: *Les liaisons pernicieuses*

The Elf Scandal, or 'L'affaire Elf', as it became known, began with a 1993 investigation by the Commission des opérations de bourse (COB, the national agency which regulates stock market activity in France). The COB inquiry was not originally directed at Elf, but at Maurice Bidermann, the head of a textile and clothing manufacturing company which had been involved in a heated lawsuit with a Bidermann associate in the United States. As information began to emerge that Bidermann had been getting clandestine infusions of financing from Elf-Aquitaine, COB realized that it had opened the lid on a potentially explosive case with possible criminal implications. The Bidermann case was passed to the French investigative authorities.

In France major investigations such as the Bidermann case are handled by an investigating magistrate known as a *juge d'instruction*. These officials act independently of the political system and have an authority that combines certain police powers with certain judicial powers. The Bidermann case was assigned to a *juge d'instruction* named Eva Joly, who took up the case with gusto. She was intrigued by Elf's use of an affiliate to channel funds to support Bidermann* and found Elf funds going in a number of directions, including into the coffers of key French political parties.

---

* Bidermann's sister had introduced Elf's CEO, Loïk Le Floch-Prigent, to his future wife (Fatima Belaïd), according to a report in the *International Herald Tribune*. The textile executive maintained a friendship with the couple and was allegedly involved in helping them settle their later widely-publicized and hostile divorce, in which Belaïd allegedly walked away with large amounts of payoffs from Elf Aquitaine. She also became a defendant in the Elf case over these payments.

1

Mr Africa

By 1996 after the collection of documents through searches of Elf and Bidermann offices, the trail led to André Tarallo, an Elf executive nicknamed 'Mr Africa' for his long-term relationships with leaders of several oil-producing countries in Africa, most of which were former French colonies. Because of its government ties, Elf Aquitaine had reportedly been used as an arm of diplomacy and espionage by the French government since the days of former president Charles de Gaulle, who is credited with implementing the system in the 1950s after the independence of France's former colonies.

Tarallo became a key figure in the Elf scandal. He had been associated with Elf since 1967, when its then CEO, Pierre Guillaumat, assigned him the task of managing the oil company's secret payments of 'commissions.' Using these payments to establish relations with the new leaders of western Africa, especially in the oil-rich country of Gabon, Tarallo became the link between the African leaders and Elf's affiliates. In the process he personally acquired great wealth. By the time the Elf scandal broke in the early 1990s, Tarallo had become known for a luxurious mansion he had acquired in his native Corsica.

In July 1996 Tarallo was charged by Judge Joly in connection with payments of over 100 million francs to Bidermann through two affiliates of Elf's unit in Gabon, known as Elf-Gabon. The following day, Elf's CEO, Loïk Le Floch-Prigent, was himself charged with abuse of corporate assets and abuse of a position of trust ('abus de biens sociaux' and 'abus de confiance'). Le Floch-Prigent was arrested the same day.

Commissions, commissions, and more commissions

By early 1997 Joly had located other dubious foreign dealings involving Elf. For example, there was a $20 million 'commission' paid by Elf to several beneficiaries in connection with a contract for Elf in Venezuela in 1992. Some of these funds passed through or into the hands of Tarallo, Alfred Sirven (who acted as a type of chief of staff to Le Floch-Prigent), and an advisor to Gabon president Omar Bongo, according to testimony from a businessman named André Guelfi, who was often used by Elf as an intermediary in the distribution of 'commissions.' Guelfi emerged as an intermediary again in connection with a 'commission' of about 44 million francs paid in 1992 by Elf involving its attempt to acquire an oil refinery in Leuna, in the former East Germany. The 44 million turned out to be only a portion of the 'commissions' received from Elf by intermediaries in the controversial Leuna project. In addition to Guelfi, these intermediaries included two former secret service agents and at least two front companies which allegedly helped channel Elf money into the coffers of the German Christian Democratic Party, which was believed to be in a position to help Elf secure approval for the Leuna acquisition. When these payments were revealed, the Elf affair spilled across the border to disrupt German politics as well.

In March 1997 Judge Joly, now joined by another investigator, Judge Laurence Vichnievsky, began looking into an instance of attempted fraud in a scheme where Elf was reportedly used in 1990 by multinational enterprise Thomson and others to induce the government of Taiwan to buy several military ships. It was this series of activities that led to the first trial in the Elf affair. In the course of this case, it was alleged that over 60 million francs had been passed around among individuals seeking to influence the decision of then French foreign minister Roland Dumas in connection with selling the ships to Taiwan.

The self-proclaimed 'Whore of the Republic'

In November 1997 businessman Gilbert Miara was charged as an intermediary in acquiring a luxury apartment in Paris with Elf funds for Dumas's mistress, Christine Deviers-Joncour, who was placed on Elf's payroll and was allegedly involved in the transfers of Elf 'commissions' to Swiss bank accounts. In January 1998 Deviers-Joncour was charged as an accomplice in the attempted fraud case involving the ship sales. By mid 1998 she was also under investigation in Switzerland. In November 1998 she offered her side of the story to the public in the form of a book entitled *The Whore of the Republic (La putain de la république)*. Over the course of the next two years she seemed to alternate between exonerating Dumas and implicating him. Both were found guilty in the first Elf trial in 2000. Dumas's conviction was later overturned on appeal.

3

Elf's financial mastermind

Meanwhile Joly and Vichnievsky continued to find dubious dealings in connection with Elf. Two of the three key Elf figures, Tarallo and Le Floch-Prigent, had already been charged, but the third, Alfred Sirven, had disappeared. Sirven was at the heart of Elf's web of secret financial channels through Switzerland and other havens. According to one report and a book on the case by French journalists Gilles Gaetner and Jean-Marie Pontaut, investigators estimated that Sirven had over a billion francs at his disposal and was the only one to really know all the details of where the money was. The two French investigators handling the case – Joly and Vichnievsky – and now joined by a third, Judge Reynaud Van Ruymbeke, sought the lifting of national security restrictions on the disclosure of Elf payments to solidify their case.

Sirven was suspected of using as many as 4,000 affiliate entities to channel Elf money around the world. His disappearance caused consternation to investigators, who issued arrest warrants through Interpol and even journeyed to South Africa after receiving credible reports that he had been spotted there. These sightings turned out to be false. In February 2001 Alfred Sirven was located and arrested in the Philippines, where he had gone into hiding with the family of a Filipino friend. He was extradited to France to stand trial.

Sirven was not the only Elf defendant who had managed to elude the investigators. In July 2000 French authorities issued a warrant for the arrest of Iraqi-British businessman Nahdmi Auchi, reputed to be among the ten wealthiest individuals in Great Britain. Auchi was suspected of receiving 'commissions' from Elf as an intermediary in its 1991 acquisition of the Ertoil petroleum refinery in Spain. According to press reports, British authorities refused to honour the arrest warrant for a year, but eventually Auchi himself consented to the extradition.

Elf II

The second Elf trial began in March 2003 with over thirty defendants. Most were convicted in a highly-publicized trial which focused on the alleged misappropriation of some 2 billion francs and resulted in prison sentences for the high-profile defendants – Le Floch-Prigent, Sirven, and

Tarallo – announced in November 2003. As the sound and fury of the case faded away, this trio of key Elf figures reportedly managed to secure their release from prison on health grounds, as the French political class breathed a sigh of relief.

On many occasions in the course of the Elf affair, the French press had hinted at the implication of high-profile politicians in some of Elf's activities. Of the politicians potentially involved, only Roland Dumas was actually charged, and his conviction was overturned. Aflred Sirven was reputed to be the only one to know all the details of the potential involvement of politicians in Elf's dealings, but if he had such information, he chose not to divulge it.

About Eva Joly

'The French media has resorted to old clichés about me, such as "the judge who came in from the cold", as if my childhood was shrouded in some kind of icy, remote or mysterious haze. As if I came from some place beyond the sun and the moon, like in the fairy tales. In fact, however, they cannot imagine how wonderful it was to grow up in the kingdom of the polar bear, and the very valuable experience it has given me. My Norwegian roots do not embarrass me, for they have provided me with most of the good things that have carried me forward in life.' These are the words of Eva Joly in the introduction to her book *Hunting Corruption* where she describes her early years in Norway.

The woman who was to become world-renowned in her profession as an investigating judge in the fight against corruption, tax evasion and money laundering,

Gro Eva Farseth was born in 1943, on the east side of Oslo, the Grüünerlöökka district, where she grew up in the shadow of the Second World War. She left home at the age of twenty and went to Paris, occupying herself on the train journey by learning French verbs; she had enrolled to study French at the Sorbonne, and the entrance exam was to take place the following day. She intended to do well, and she did. She became an au pair with the Joly family in Paris, and she studied. The eldest son of the house, Pascal, was a 23-year-old medical student, and it was love at first sight. They married despite his parents' objections. Eva Joly was starting a new life. Eva's father, Eyvind Farseth, worked as a tailor most of his life; her mother looked after the home, helped the children with their homework and her husband with the tailoring. Gro Eva was the eldest of three siblings. Her childhood was a carefree one where music, travelling and the simple things in life were celebrated.

Eva's education in Norway was a traditional one, and she took occasional jobs in her spare time. According to Eva, this is how she became independent financially, as there was no extra money at home to spend on things that weren't strictly necessary. Eva was no different from other girls her age in that she was keen to follow fashion, buy magazines, books and records. Her first job was serving behind the counter in a bakery on Karl Johan, the main street in Oslo; she worked every Saturday as well as a few hours during the week, after school. The hourly rate was three Norwegian kronas. Eva went to business college and learnt how to type. She did well in her studies and her typing speed was 200 characters per minute. During this time she also attended lectures on philosophy; this has remained an interest ever since.

Eva was aware early on of the strong links that bound the women in her family. Her maternal great-grandmother, her grandmother and her mother were all incredibly capable women. Her great-grandmother was very keen on education; her grandmother was a professional hairdresser; her mother studied German, English and French, and helped in the hairdressing salon. 'I realised at an early age how important the women in the family were, that they were the ones who maintained its traditions,' Eva says. 'We create our own family history, and each of us is the author of her own destiny. I understood how you work with what you've got and carry it forward into life. You could call it adding colour to the blank pages you are allocated in life.'

By now, Eva had decided to make her dream of travelling to France come true. She and her friends had watched many French films, and to her France seemed like the promised land, where everything was so much easier than she had hitherto experienced. She saved every penny and was lucky enough to win 1500 kronas in an essay competition about the Norwegian export business.

On a cold February day in 1964, a small group of people loaded with numerous suitcases and parcels gathered at the main railway station in Oslo. This was not Eva's first trip abroad, but her anticipation was great as she had never gone anywhere on her own. For six months she would not see her family, for six months she would have to fend for herself, for six months she would have only herself to rely on. There was, however, no sadness at the moment of parting, as with her baggage she took plenty of independence, mettle and courage, qualities that had been emphasized so very much in her upbringing. Safe journey to Paris, said her parents and siblings, and good luck.

What nobody realised, least of all Eva herself, was that she was to put down roots in France, only returning to Norway on short visits. 'I found Paris cold and dirty when I got there after a 36-hour train journey, in spite of the fact that I was used to the colder climate of Norway,' Eva says at one point. 'The city was somehow so enormous all around me. Oslo paled by comparison. Paris stretched out in front of your eyes. There was such noise: the traffic, the crowds of people wandering down avenues and narrow lanes, the street markets with people shouting at each other. Then there was the Seine flowing under illuminated bridge arches, the busy coffee bars and the labyrinths of the Métro.'

The Joly family lived right by the Jardins du Luxembourg in Paris. He was a very busy surgeon, she a housewife. Both were rich and beautiful, and they had four children of whom Pascal was the second oldest. Eva was there to help with the housework and act as a companion to the family. When Pascal and Eva started courting, his family did its utmost to drive them apart, but without success. 'When I learned that Pascal was going to bury Eva,' her father-in-law said during the wedding reception. 'Heavens above, is that how they see it?' Eva thought to herself at this stumble over the word 'marry'.

The young couple were provided with a twenty-square-metre flat at the top of the Joly family house. Pascal continued his medical studies. Eva got a secretarial job, but she was also a clever seamstress and exploited this talent as well. Presently she decided to do some further studies. She chose to read law by chance: she had meant to study medicine, but was told that studying law would be easier if she wanted to continue working. She was the breadwinner. Around this time their daughter was born.

When Pascal finished his studies he got a position at Bouray, just outside Paris, and this is where the family moved at Easter in 1973. Eva completed her studies, and became employed as a lawyer at France's largest psychiatric hospital, where she looked after the legal interests of patients who had been compulsorily confined. She worked with doctors, nurses, non-professionals and the hospital administrators. 'The insight I gained there of people and politics was an invaluable experience,' Eva said later. Some eighteen months after she started to work at the hospital their son was born, and life continued its course. In 1980, the year when Eva was 37, she started thinking about moving on. That winter there were posters everywhere which read: 'Judges needed, why not try it and do something exciting?' Why not indeed? thought Eva. She fulfilled the requirements for the job and applied for it.

There were aural and written exams, lasting a week. There were 1100 applicants for 100 positions. The last examination was very French. All applicants were called one by one before a Grand Jury. There were 15 men sitting in a row before the applicants, conservatively dressed. The questions came fast in machine-gun bursts, and the main thing was to answer quickly and keep going. She was asked about the reforms in the law relating to psychiatric wards and about divorce law.

Then came:

'What does the Kiss mean to you?'

'An expression of an emotion'

'So, you haven't heard about Rodin?'

'Haven't you heard about Vigeland, Rodin's pupil, and his great Cycle of Life?'

'What is a male chauvinist?'

'A dying breed.'

She was given the position of prosecutor in Orléans, a 90-kilometre journey from Bouray. Her working day was long and the tasks varied. The prosecutor is in charge of investigations into whatever crops up: burglaries, robberies, rapes, murders, fires, car and air accidents, and so on.

After four years in Orléans she applied for, and was appointed to, the prosecutorship in Evry, much closer to her home and family. The crime rate was worse in Evry than in Orléans; there was high unemployment, a large part of the population were immigrants and the police force was far too small to cope with the situation.

Pressure of work was a good deal greater and Eva was given even more responsibility, before long becoming head of the Fraud Division. Within a few years, however, Eva became restless, feeling that the Court in Evry lacked efficiency. She wanted a change, and took a job with the Comité Interministériel de Restructuration Industrielle (CIRI), which is under the auspices of the Ministry of Finance. They needed someone with specialized knowledge of the insolvency laws; CIRI's remit was to save companies from bankruptcy, help them find new markets and get them back on their feet. Eva was happy in her new job and, before long, had risen to become Assistant General Secretary – the first judge to be given this position, the first woman and definitely the first Norwegian au pair girl. And so Eva hung up her judge's robes for a few years. She knew, however, that she could not get any further at CIRI, and after three years thought about finding a suitable job in business to earn some money. It might, however, not be so easy finding a new career path for a woman of fifty.

Experience had taught her that there were exciting and interesting jobs in the public sector, and after much thought she decided that she wanted to go back to being a judge. She was not, however, prepared to take just anything – she wanted to put the knowledge she had gained about the world of finance to good use.

She presented herself at the office of the President of the Supreme Court. Though he was not entirely convinced of the need to create a position for her as investigating judge in the Financial Division, she was persuasive, and he agreed to give it a go. The Ministry of Justice agreed to the suggestion and Eva Joly was employed as an investigating judge as of January 1st 1993. Things, however, moved very slowly; to begin with she had no office, no desk, no telephone, and had to use one corner of a colleague's desk.

The Palais de Justice, the courthouse in the centre of Paris, near Notre-Dame, now became Eva's place of work. The office she was eventually allocated was small and badly equipped, and she soon gave up struggling with the tentacles of French bureaucracy, bringing instead a computer from home as well as cordless and mobile telephones, so that she would be accessible at all times to the police and her colleagues – a prerequisite for the job, she thought. It was fortunate that no major cases were pending during the weeks it took her to create a decent working environment for herself: each day was a battle – if she needed a pencil, or a folder in which to file the cases she was working on, she had to write a request in triplicate justifying the need. Eva's attitude was to go herself and buy whatever she needed rather than spend her working days on hopeless bickering. The change from CIRI was considerable. There, people had been appreciated and problems were tackled straightaway whereas in the Ministry of Justice, staff were looked upon as spendthrifts and pencil-chewers.

One day she felt she had had enough and without warning her superior, the Justice Minister Elisabeth Guigou, she summoned the media to show them her working conditions. The Minister was less than thrilled and said she couldn't bear 'media judges'. But Eva got what she wanted. Her department was moved to large and well-appointed offices. At last the French were taking financial crime seriously.

Eva's first cases were relatively simple. A hedonist who sold his soul for sports cars (investigation revealed he had charged the cars to his employers); a stockbroker who had an extravagant lifestyle (investigation revealed he had fiddled the firm's end-of-year accounts and cheated its customers). Eva worked well with the police, getting major support from the Assistant Commissioner, a former detective. Together, they instigated new procedures to counter fraud, treating it on a par with other serious crimes and using similar methods to deal with it: phone-tapping, house searches, police interrogations, imprisonment and detention, all according to what was needed. A forceful investigating judge inspires the police force. What matters is to make people understand that financial crimes are as serious as other crimes.

It was during the spring of 1994 that Eva got her first big case, the Bernard Tapie case, and became famous overnight. Tapie, one of France's most prominent citizens, was perhaps the first to experience Eva Joly's new working methods. Originally a pop singer, he had gone into business and was at one time perhaps best known for owning the French football club Marseille. Tapie was a Member of Parliament, and was for a while a minister in the government of Francois Mitterrand. When Eva began to study his papers, it transpired that he was a tax evader who used taxpayers' money for his own benefit and was deep in all kinds of fraudulent activities. Tapie enjoyed parliamentary privilege, but Eva had it lifted, imposed a travel ban and had him brought in handcuffs for interrogation. Never before had a 'white-collar' person been treated in such a way. Such cases, if indeed they ever reached court, had hitherto usually been dismissed. The media had a field day, but this case only served to strengthen the bond between investigating judge and the police. Her determination won the day, and Tapie was given an 18-month sentence, of which six were unconditional.

Eva Joly works as a special adviser on fraud for the Norwegian government. Her fame has not stopped Eva Joly from continuing to be just as passionate as ever about her work. As always, she is still the last one to leave the office, and remains a familiar figure to her colleagues, buried behind enormous piles of documents with her reading glasses perched on her nose. Eva Joly's star was to shine even brighter with the so-called Elf case. The oil giant Elf-Aquitaine, owned by the French state, had been systematically bled dry by government officials. This involved vast amounts of slush money, bribery and corruption, tax evasion and misuse of public funds. But that is another story.

Eva Joly now lives on her own. Her husband died in 2001 (they had divorced three years earlier). Their two children carry on with their own lives, she a lawyer and he an architect.

Ouverture

I am writing this book in a log cabin in the mountains. The house is built on land that belonged to my forebears when they were peasants. It's a very vivid link to those previous generations, when it was such a struggle to survive. Our present opulence shouldn't make us forget that our great-grandparents lived in a world as tough as the favelas of Brazil, the slums of Mexico or the plains of Szechuan still are today.

A friend often lets me have the key to this, her *hütte*, since I've come back to live in Norway. The dimensions of the room where I'm working on this book were dictated by the size of the tree trunks that were available at the time. All around, only the occasional turf-roofed alpine farm occupies this high peat plateau covered with what the Norwegians call marsh wool: swathes of wild grass, which bend before the wind. Outside, it feels like I'm on the edge of the world. The elks and the birds of prey are the true lords of these mountains covered with heather, juniper and bilberries. They merely tolerate our presence.

In the sunless Scandinavian winters, the cold can kill a human being in less than six hours. So, in Norwegian, the expression 'to spend a winter's night in the open' means to survive a fearsome challenge.

In my own way, I have spent a winter's night in the open. I have been threatened with death, just for doing my job. I went about my daily business under the close surveillance of the secret service and other agencies, subjected to the sort of pressure that I could never have imagined: I have been vilified and accused of the worst sorts of wrongdoing, almost as if justice itself were the guilty party. There is no point in endlessly asking oneself why and how. Whenever, as a judge, you get close to those in power, whether it's official power or covert power, you are caught up in something much greater than yourself. That is the way it is.

But when the storm breaks over you, when you are continuously manipulated and intimidated, when such powerful forces rise up against you, words no longer have exactly the same meaning. Because you are the target.

Of course I wasn't alone in the eye of the storm. We were a handful of judges, police and legal administrators struggling against a fearsome headwind. Logically, our efforts should have been encouraged and progressed by successive governments. But our investigations were under constant surveillance and were sometimes undermined. The establishment did not protect us as much as it should have from the pressures and violent manipulation which were brought to bear on us. Sometimes it even encouraged discord in the heart of our teams, almost as if it had deliberately chosen to torpedo our work.

When, in order to get on with one's task, one can only count on one's endurance, perseverance and ability to rise above distraction, sooner or later the rope will always break.

During the last months of the Elf investigation, I was only holding on by a thread. The fact that I managed to hold on, and get out safely from a very tense case that I was able to see through to the finish had nothing to do with me personally. It's rather that what I saw and understood gave me a sense of responsibility towards my fellow human beings.

In this little shack of a house, where all you need to get through the day is a few logs, some tea and a few potatoes, the conflict seems unevenly balanced. It seems ridiculous to be writing in a little mountain hut about the masters of high finance, those shadowy figures with private jets who frequent the palaces of the capital cities of Europe, for whom a million-dollar commission is just a tip, those men who rise and fall in the sophisticated universe of offshore-based companies, who disappear in the padded silence of the administration.

I could stay here forever and just melt away into the mountains. The course of events wouldn't change one bit. But there is a tradition in Norway. For centuries, at the birth of a child, two or three hundred pine trees were marked out in the forest. They were then topped out so that the trunks would grow straighter and thicker. These trees were reserved for the child's future house. The woodcutters were preparing for its future.

This book is inspired by that tradition. We are contemporaries; we are travelling together. None of us is contented to live in isolation, in a bubble, guided only by self-interest, shut off from any horizon other than one's own. Life is other people. The plague I have uncovered during the course of my work, and of which I have experienced only the beginning, does not yet have a name. Out of habit we use words like 'corruption' or 'financial impropriety'. I would rather use the word 'impunity'; a way of living above the law, because one is stronger than the law.

The world has turned upside down. What economy can carry on for long without trust? What democracy can survive if the elite has both the power to violate the law and the guarantee of impunity?

And yet, fatalism and impotence take over: like those black tides which, winter after winter, discharge their lethal cargoes on the Atlantic coasts of Europe, without one knowing anything about it save through the empty declarations of those seemingly managerless petrol companies, whose directors hide behind front companies in the Bahamas, Zug or Malta. Scandal follows scandal. You get immune to it. The feeling is that nothing's going to change, so let's talk about something else. Cynicism gains ground.

I refuse to accept this. We can still stop our children from growing up in a world where impunity rules among the powerful, where only ordinary folk have duties. Our children do not deserve that. If we let the world order fall apart, whether our children grow up in New York, in Buenos Aires, in the suburbs of Kyoto or somewhere along the Rhine, they will be living, without realising it, under the rule of unknown masters who are both unjust and invisible.

This story is a universal one, but it is also my story. By becoming a magistrate, I agreed to fight for justice in the name of the people. This account is for them. My story, modest though it may be, belongs to them, not to me. Thus, what I am doing today would be incomprehensible if I had not crossed these bridges.

A Worry

Destiny is not something that can be contained. It knocks at your door without warning, even when swooping on an investigating magistrate, an anonymous cog in the aged legal machine.

It was a morning like any other. Sunnier, perhaps; near the end of winter. The Palais de Justice in Paris, a sublime building nestled in the embrace of the slate-grey Seine, had rarely seemed so pretty. Behind its lofty façade, it's an anthill. My office was a cupboard hidden away at the end of a maze. Eight usable square metres out of a nominal thirteen. Walls of files. An old manual typewriter on the table. A grey lamp with a 60-watt bulb and a temperamental switch. The walls of the Palais de Justice have seen regimes come and go; time has long ago caught up with its labyrinthine corridors and monumental rooms, with their stucco and carvings, decorated with allegorical frescoes. In the old democracies of the world, the bureaucracy sets up its filing cabinets and dusty telephones in monumental buildings, like a vestige of past splendours.

Since I arrived in the Ministry of Finance, after a rewarding assignment in the Treasury[1] – the best of the French administration – I had experienced the very worst of it. I went from disappointment to disappointment. Almost every day the judicial administration seemed to make an absurd decision; like the Shadocks, popular cartoon characters in France, whose motto is, 'Why make things simple when you can make them complicated?'

Thankfully, my programme for the morning cheered me up. I was due to review the current investigations with the police financial investigation

---

1   As magistrate seconded to the Interministerial Committee for Industrial Reconstruction.

division. I love opportunities to work with a team; it makes a change from being alone with the files. Since my very earliest days as a judge, I've got on extraordinarily well with the police. We have the same pragmatic approach; a belief that the thorough examination of a heating bill or a diary tends to reveal many more secrets than lengthy intellectual deduction. The devil is in the detail.

On this particular day, we went through the current investigations in order. We went through each file at a gallop. The Bidermann affair appeared on the top of the pile. The police investigations were just ticking over; it was a routine procedure.[2] None of us was particularly inspired by the file. The suspicious bailing-out of a textile company, even by the number one company in France[3] didn't really pique our curiosity. That winter I was investigating more important matters. The Ciments Français affair, which aroused strong suspicions of insider trading and false accounting, was using all my resources. However, a small spark was lit during the course of our discussion. Overcomplicated financial arrangements, strange patterns of transactions… Experience gives you reflexes. Intuition is a muscle which you strengthen, case by case. The tiny details added up to something intriguing and I wanted to find out the truth. I decided that the investigation needed to be sped up, and issued fresh instructions. And then we moved on to the next matter.

I now know that on that day, somewhere in Paris, fresh worry lines appeared on the already wrinkled foreheads of some powerful men. These were the very same lines I saw appear so often on the foreheads of witnesses, in my chambers, when they were giving their statements. I had become a worry to them.

I knew nothing of this. From the very beginning, there was a gap between the disquiet the investigation caused and my perception of the case. This delayed reaction would be a defining characteristic of the investigation. I would never quite close the gap. Of course, one is tempted to revisit events in the light of what one learned afterwards. But that's hindsight, and a falsifying of the truth. How, at that moment, could I have

2   On 18th August 1994, following an inquiry and the receipt of a dossier by the Commission for Stock Market Operations, the public prosecutor's department opened a preliminary investigation, which was made the responsibility of my chambers, to deal with the financial undertakings – seemingly excessive and partially concealed – made by the petroleum company Elf-Aquitaine to the Bidermann group.
3   As at 31st December 1993, the Elf group was number one in France, with a turnover of 209 thousand million francs, or 31.86 thousand million euros.

imagined that the misappropriations that were coming to light would finally add up to several billion francs, and that as a result some 37 people would be put formally under examination as a preliminary indictment and sent to the criminal court?

How could I have imagined that, seven years later, instead of that thin yellow folder that we opened that winter morning, the file would comprise more than 100,000 pages, 850 sealed packages of evidence (nearly ten cubic metres of it), and 256 volumes?[4]

This is the story that has to be told. More than the facts themselves, the conditions in which we undertook our inquiry show an underground world which escapes ordinary justice and considers the law a mug's game.

To know what it costs

To retrace the detail of our investigations would be unworthy of the mandate I had been given. The outline of them was made public during the three months of the Elf trial. But as I write these words, the final verdict has not been reached. I could write at length about legal confidentiality. I've been able to see how it has become legal fiction. But it still forms part of the Penal Code, and at the age of 58, I am not about to start violating that code, which I was charged with upholding throughout my career.

On the other hand, whilst justice needs calm and quiet in order to function, it shouldn't accept being pushed into the shadows. The threats and intimidation of which I was the target during all these years of inquiry are not covered by any professional code. Nowhere is it written in the code of penal procedure that a judge, by virtue of their position, should be the object of never-ending rumour, unauthorised phone-taps or openly Mafioso 'advice'. No one includes in their oath of office that they should be afraid to open their own front door. Nor that they will take repeated insults and interference without retaliating.

It would be very odd if the violent tactics which I have had to deal with were to remain hidden behind legal confidentiality. Until I am proved wrong, I believe that this exists in order to protect investigations and not

---

4   When it was electronically scanned, the dossier on 17th March 2003, the first day of the Elf trial, filled the equivalent of two DVDs, or ten CD-ROMs.

those who wish to interfere with them. If the latter thought they could freely pile provocation upon intimidation under the protective wing of professional confidentiality, they were wrong. My freedom of expression is constitutionally guaranteed, as is any other European citizen's.

Likewise, the obligation to a degree of professional reserve is not a masochistic commandment that transforms everyone who works for the state into a Saint Sebastian riddled with arrows. My honour has been publicly attacked and my professional integrity questioned. I have decided to use my right to speak out because this story is the foundation of my current post with the Norwegian government. Rolling back the frontiers of impunity is not a slogan: you have to know what it costs.

I have chosen in this book, most of the time, to conceal the names of my interlocutors, sometimes because of legal confidentiality, but most often in order not to put them in the firing line. I am going to tell my tale by means of successive flashbacks, each of which has implications beyond the bounds of the investigation itself. But it's sometimes impossible for me to separate entirely the events from the context within which they took place. What I write has to be verifiable. The threats that I received and the size of the obstacles which were put in our way have to be exposed clearly so that the reader can freely form their own opinion.

This book also comes with another warning. An inquiry is not a story which unfolds in a linear manner; it is a succession of sometimes contradictory truths. Something which seems an established fact one day can be contradicted a year later. A request for banking information from abroad, which can take two to three years to complete, can cast fresh light on previous hearings. This painstaking working out of judicial information is made even more complex once one starts dealing with economic offences. The legal and technical sophistication of financial arrangements do not make this story easy. Chronology's sole virtue is convenience: it doesn't at all reflect the final image of the case.

A smouldering fire

Spring 1995. Our inquiry meeting at the Palais de Justice a few weeks earlier had been fruitful. As we dipped into the first indicators at our disposal, the re-floating of the Bidermann Group was beginning to look rather different. Each day we pulled a little more on the piece of wool, and the whole ball was beginning to unravel. Funds from Elf-Gabon[5] were appearing in the accounts of the textile firm. More than an industrial decision, this arrangement could hide a secret agreement. Still without entirely realising it, behind a few surface anomalies, we had entered into a labyrinth of companies, false ceilings, deceptive appearances and, some real trafficking.[6]

Thus far, thankfully, the affair only featured in a few brief snippets in the newspapers, lost amongst swathes of other articles. But I could feel that a fire was smouldering in my office, and I could already sense that it was of another nature. I interviewed numerous direct or indirect witnesses to the contentious facts. I could see a discrepancy between the elements in the file, which were still fairly small fry, and the tense climate which surrounded this story.

I witnessed the past catching up with solid figures torn from the business world. Surprised, I watched them by turns go pale, trip over their words, sweat and become breathless. Their gaze would slip away and cast desperately over the bookshelf, the files and their labels handwritten in black ink and red felt-tip pen, looking for reassurance. Fear is an uncontrollable emotion, a vertiginous emotion against which you can battle step by step but which will always end up drowning you. No one can pretend that they are feeling it, and I felt that they weren't play-acting.

Their tales continued, each one more amazing than the last. They told of direct death threats, of night-time nuisance phone calls, of sabotaged vehicles, of break-ins designed purely to intimidate, where nothing was taken but the apartment was turned upside down, of rumours of assassinations gleefully put about as if they were disguised warnings…

Of course, I know that the world of an oil giant is nothing like a Roald Dahl story. Most of the world's commercial oilfields are to be found in the Middle East, West Africa and South America, whilst the greatest oil tycoons of the world are westerners. Black gold is not a simple formula. The discovery of oil and its exploitation represent a bloody story 'told by an idiot, full of sound and fury' about which Shakespeare would have

---

5   One of the subsidiaries of Elf, with enormous assets and special status because it was half-owned by the state of Gabon.
6   On 21st April 1995, even though the inquiry had already yielded its first fruits, the board of Elf brought an action against X in this connection.

written a play if he had lived in our times; a succession of subterfuges and coups d'état, of hidden movements of funds and of pacts with the devil.

The men of the oil industry live in a world where the customs bear little resemblance to the rest of the world. Thus we have a former refinery director, an Elf employee, who worked for a long time in hostile territories; a well-toughened character, solid as a rock. One day he casually mentions a letter, which he had given to his lawyer several months before the beginning of the investigation, in which he explained that if he ever had an accident, it would be an assassination. I read the letter: it named his own managers as the potential threat. That is how these men live.

'Elf's people on the pavement'

The file that I was examining is a financial affair on French soil, with protagonists who had, at that time, nothing to do with defence secrets. Nonetheless, the methods which we uncovered should be inconceivable in a democratic country. In peacetime, men and women living in the heart of leafy areas of Paris, in sumptuous apartments giving on to dreamlike avenues, were as fearful as fugitives hunted by a gang in a wasteland. When they were walking up stairs, they slowed down as they neared the top for fear of seeing a shadow appear there. They never got into their cars without being apprehensive. They never used the phone. Their apartments were searched.

I went through endless transcripts, reports, contracts and extracts from bank accounts, feeling like I was in a shoddy thriller, with one obvious difference of scale: these men and women feared the police because their pursuers had infiltrated the police force. And they had no confidence in the institutions of state, because their enemies wielded even greater power.

I do not share their fear; I am simply recording it. A judge is like a doctor who, having seen several patients, is no longer bothered by the sight of blood. The violence which infiltrated my investigating chambers is composed of the facts and the witness statements which accumulated there. It doesn't concern me – not any more, anyway.

The first few months were like the skies of the Ile de France before the rain – a few white filaments before the slow but inexorable rise of a black veil presaging the downpour. One evening, after a witness hearing with an Elf engineer, I realised that the clouds had gathered above my head. During his career, this man had resisted his superiors and refused to carry out orders which seemed to him to be unlawful. He had accepted the consequences of this, which were inevitable in his world: anonymous warnings, rumours that he was unstable and direct death threats.

The hearing finished. I sat alone for a few moments. So as to have something to do with my hands whilst I reflected, I tidied up the papers spread over my desk. Suddenly, my witness reappeared at the door. I made a surprised gesture. Immediately, he put a finger to his lips, signalling to me not to react. He took one of the sheets of paper on my desk and scribbled, 'Look out! I've seen Elf's people on the pavement outside.' He looked at me for a few seconds and then left again.

I understood straight away what was going on. This man had seen it all before. He had not become a senior executive by being content to whistle blithely across the Pont de Neuilly on his way to the Elf office in the Défense. He knew the hidden agenda. He knew what he was doing. I understood that he was showing me that my office was not secure, and that my work was undoubtedly under surveillance.

In the line of fire

The unsavoury reputation of the oil giants in the areas of intelligence or clandestine activity is well known, whether you're talking about the former 'seven sisters' owned by British, Dutch and American companies, or their French cousins. For Elf, this underhand dimension is built into its genes. Its founder, Pierre Guillaumat, was in charge of the French secret services in London during the Second World War. He was subsequently Defence Minister and responsible for the atomic weapons programme. It is common knowledge that, from the outset, he positioned people, at all levels, whose responsibilities were twofold: oil executive and intelligence agent. Elf maintained an autonomous intelligence service, officially charged with the protection of its installations.[7] In the 1980s, this dimension grew with the explosion of commission payments given to

---

7   At the beginning of the 1960s, Pierre Guillaumat gave the general secretariat of the petroleum group an information cell supervised by a special services agent in permanent contact with General de Gaulle's advisor for African affairs, Jacques Foccart. During successive decades, the security of Elf stayed in the hands of the secret services, whether under the direction of Colonel Maurice Robert, co-founder with

25

'intermediaries' who were supposed to facilitate the successful closing of contracts, which sometimes concealed diplomatic arrangements and the corruption of foreign governments. In this world there were some rather disreputable characters, both in France and Africa.

In this way, successive networks were laid down over the organisation of the firm like so many sedimentary layers. Being in their line of fire was not a particularly pleasant prospect.

That little scribble on the piece of paper was my first worrying incident. I had already received several threats whilst working on a previous investigation. But this incident suddenly made real the tense atmosphere which had pervaded the previous weeks' hearings. I remembered the threats reported by the witnesses: 'You're going to get a bullet in the back', 'If you don't do what you're told, something nasty will happen to you', 'He told me to be careful crossing the road'... The meaning of these warnings suddenly became crystal clear.

Compared to what I had to live through afterwards, the fear I felt that day seems to be disproportionate. But with work like these there isn't a Richter scale. You just notice trouble. In the evening, head leaning against the window of the commuter train which was taking me homewards, events jostled for my attention. I mulled things over, putting the different parts of the puzzle into place. And I decided to continue to live as normal, without letting fear enter into my life.

If my concerns had triumphed over me, I could have discreetly closed the investigation, without making any waves. No one would have known. The world would have continued to turn. I would have plunged back into suspect bankruptcies and fiscal fraud, with a bit of credit card fraud thrown in. When I look at the opprobrium which I had to face up to later, and think that I had to risk my life, when I measure the price that we all had to pay, I wonder if the end was worth the means.

But 'I could have' and 'I should have' are not expressions that I like. French is a language which plays with the uncertainty of feelings. It cultivates the conditional or the future anterior, those national subtleties. I am more prosaic, more concrete, more Norwegian deep down. There

---

Jacques Foccart of the African branch of the French Intelligence Service, or of Patrice de Loustal, who directed the Action service of the French Intelligence and Espionage Service, or of Jean-Pierre Daniel, nicknamed 'the Colonel', an ex-secret service officer. (cf. 'L'étrange interpenetration des service d'Elf et de la France' *Le Monde*, 28th September 1997).

could be no question of letting myself be intimidated. If I was now a worry to them, I would become a real danger.

Threats

The affair was not yet a year old when I received my first messenger.

In the world of sensitive politics, the secret services and the paramilitary police, language is coded and oblique. An agent from the internal state security department, the CIA or Mossad doesn't knock on your door to explain to your face what he's dealing with nor what he thinks of your actions. He uses intermediaries who pass on messages sufficiently sibylline that they say things without actually spelling them out.

The first messenger was called Franz – or at least that was what he called himself. He was introduced to me by a friend. For several months I had been caught up in a bit of a social whirl. A recent acquaintance invited me to go to the theatre with his circle of friends. I took his attentiveness for a casual enjoyment of being together, visiting refined exhibitions, going to delightful concerts and, of course, this being Paris, dining with each other.

One evening, this friend invited me to a party at his house. I accepted straight away: as the pressure around the investigation grew, I was grabbing every opportunity for going out, to refresh my mind and smell the outdoors. After some minutes a man broke away from a group. My friend introduced him to me as Franz. The stranger took me to one side. In a tone of voice that was simultaneously caressing yet firm, befitting a shadowy figure, he warned me, 'Madame, you have to understand that 98% of offences can be brought to court. But there are 2% that the legal system cannot deal with. That 2% are state secrets. There are many powerful interests around you. Take care. The state has people to guard its secrets. And they are not gentle. You have to be reasonable...'

Alarm bells were ringing in my head. I understood that my friendship had been used. I didn't say anything, just listened, and from the following day I let a distance grow between that little group and myself. I would learn some years later that our mutual friend, not meaning any harm, was part of a circle which included one of the most important people questioned in connection with the Elf case. He had just been the messenger.

The lesser of two evils

The pressure cooker was in place. I could even hear the clicks of the mechanism as it tightened. I understood that I had to be just as vigilant outside the Palais de Justice, and that this investigation was going to have repercussions on my personal life. Henceforth, I would be on my guard.

I also understood the message: that there was a line which was not to be crossed. I agreed entirely. I had no illusions: with three and a half people (a clerk of the court and two inspectors from the financial investigation division, one of whom was part-time), we were not going to start a revolution and bring down a system which looked more and more as if it had been created and encouraged at the highest level of the Republic. I had my own ideas about the limits that should not be crossed, and it was entirely possible that they were not the same as theirs.

When my colleagues told me to be careful, I answered that being weak never won anything. My instincts were telling me to take action. I had enough proof that offences had been committed. I was in the midst of something strange. There was no reason for me to halt my investigations: on the contrary, the obstacles almost reinforced my determination.

However, willpower must not get confused with recklessness. A warning light was now permanently on in the back of my mind. I was not investigating a standard case. I discovered that the firm had been organised in a sophisticated way, restricting knowledge of the in's and out's of the oil contracts to a few key people. In the bewildering jungle of Elf's organisation, with its innumerable off-shoots, its official hierarchy and an entirely parallel power structure, I felt like I was going into an unknown country, with its own laws: a collection of informal rules with a great deal left unsaid. Because General de Gaulle had wished it so, Elf was a lever for French diplomacy. In the course of the inquiry, I could well step on a mine, one of those secrets which are not the responsibility of the law.

In government, there are subjects which in effect escape the light of democracy: parallel negotiations, covert agreements which mean that 'sensible' countries can be supplied with arms, or secret alliances between states which no one is empowered to make public. As a citizen, one can regret this. But as a magistrate, it is impossible for me to conceal it. Our country has kept interests in its former African colonies; France is the third greatest exporter of arms in the world, a major player in the nuclear game and a permanent member of the UN Security Council, with all the underground activity that accompanies such status.

I had to account for the submerged part of the iceberg in my work. Therefore, I enrolled in a course at the Institut des Hautes Etudes de Défense Nationale.[1] As I was carrying out an inquiry in an area where corruption threatened the State, I thought I might as well widen my horizons and learn about things which are not in the penal code or commercial law. France has created some marvellous institutions, of which the IHEDN is one. For a year, I had the privilege of attending first-class lectures, as part of an audience of handpicked listeners. If need be, it seemed to me that there was always among my classmates a messenger to join me if I got a little too close to matters which were not the concern of a judge.

Sensitive cases require a political and collective approach. I deliberately stress 'political' and not 'partisan'. A collegiate dimension is essential. I often refer back to my experience in the Treasury in this respect. Our committee looked into the restructuring of failing companies. We often had to choose between several unattractive options to find an acceptable solution, which often came down to finding the lesser of two evils. The important thing was that the companies survived and overcame the trauma of bankruptcy.

I still bear the marks of those years. I knew that we had to make decisions based on experience rather than learned from textbooks. So I constantly shared any information I had with the public prosecutor's

---

1 Created in 1949, the IHEDN seeks to give French leaders, particularly those in the public sector, the armed forces and sensitive industries, a deeper insight into national defence as it is understood in the widest sense. In 1997 the IHEDN became a public administrative establishment and is under the control of the prime minister.

office, which given my level, cooperated with me.[2] We found common ground: I could concentrate on the concrete elements which might constitute offences, neglecting none of them, without ever letting myself be fooled by the rumours which were stirred up in my team, like the *muleta* that distracts the bull's attention in the ring.

Unexpected resistance

An investigating magistrate is sometimes wrongly described by those detractors of French justice as a solitary Savonarola[3], entrusted with a purifying mission, shut away in the ivory tower of the case in question. This is just as inaccurate as the common caricature of the 'little person' who triumphs over the powerful. Because the judge is not alone.

Napoleon's description of the investigating magistrate as 'the most powerful man in France' is wrong too. There is of course a measure of truth in it: on paper, regarding my jurisdiction,[4] I had considerable powers, ranging from that of being able to order searches to placing suspects under provisional detention.[5] But French institutions rely on a complex system of checks and balances between the magistrates, which provides a good guarantee against individual mavericks.

In a sensitive affair, an investigating magistrate can, of course, go off on his own. But that's a dead end. If he goes ahead with his inquiries, waging an open war against the public prosecutor's office, if the institution does

---

2   The French legal system distinguishes on the one hand between the judges of the bench, who have tenure and are independent, and are charged with preliminary investigations and sentencing and on the other the magistrates from the public prosecutor's department, working under the Chancellor's department. They are charged with seeing through the application of the law and keeping a watch on the general interests of society. The freedom of action of the investigating magistrate is controlled by the public prosecutor's office, which can refer the investigating office to the requisite appeal court to annul certain of its actions or expedite others.

3   Crusading Dominican friar who drove the Medici family out of Florence. He was later excommunicated and executed for criticizing Pope Alexander VI.

4   An investigating magistrate may only start investigations following a so-called 'introductory' arraignment from the Attorney-General, which presents the facts to be looked at by the preliminary inquiry (article 80 of the code of penal procedure). If new criminal facts are brought to the attention of the investigating magistrate, he or she must communicate them immediately to the public prosecutor's department, from which he or she may request an extension of referral by means of a supplementary arraignment.

5   From the beginning, the investigating manager has the prerogative of putting someone who has been indicted into provisional detention, on certain conditions and under the control of the public prosecutor's department. Since the introduction of the law of 15th June 2000, this task has been devolved to the judge responsible for release and detention.

not pass on his work, at the very least the case will indubitably finish up in the bowels of the Palais de Justice, where annulled or blocked procedures rejected by the system pile up.

From the outset I set myself an important limit: my investigations had to be accepted and supported by my peers, even if the institution to which I belonged spluttered and dragged its feet along the way, because I was pushing at doors which were normally left carefully closed. I would always follow this course. My objective was to bring before the court only that which could be tried, and to be content with this result, without exhausting myself with chimaeras. I could not, from my office, pick a battle with the state.

My opinion on this matter would not change in eight years. Circumstances, however, would; at each stage, the machinery of this turbulent inquiry would take us a little further than we had originally imagined. It is true that the reactions of the directors under investigation were irrational. In their world, peopled with important politicians and figures from the financial sector, the law exists only in an incidental way. The law has to adjust to their behaviour, and not the other way around. They live in a world without restrictions, where the only things that count are a blank cheque from the boss and the law of the cunning: what the eye doesn't see the heart doesn't grieve over.

Instead of arguing coolly, taking advantage of our initial naivety and the cumbersome nature of the law, they decided to take a forceful approach: manipulation and strong-arm tactics. They thought I would bend and submit. However, even though I flexed, trembled, hesitated and got things wrong sometimes, I did not give up. Sometimes their threats even redoubled our efforts, which was manifestly something they hadn't anticipated.

Arriving at work one morning, I found a little green visiting card. It was in the transparent plastic envelope stuck to the door of my office, number 126, which we normally used to hold a sign saying that hearings were in progress so that no one would barge in.

But this card was not of the regulation type. I could make out a list of names written in pencil, of which I recognised only the first; that of Judge Renaud.[6] The other names, I found out later, were those of French

---

6   Francois Renaud, an investigating magistrate in Lyons, one of the founders of the magistrates' trade union, was executed in the middle of the street by a team of three killers, on the night of 2nd /3rd July 1975, when he was coming back from an evening with a friend. The crime has never been solved.

magistrates killed since the war. All of them were crossed out apart from mine.

During the following hours, it was difficult for me to concentrate properly on my job. My mind ran wild, assailed by a thousand thoughts, whilst disgust and anger mounted up in me. If they thought that this kind of provocation would stop me, they were mistaken.

Around my house

May 1996. After eighteen months of intensive investigation, the case entered a decisive phase and began to centre on the previous chairman and managing director of Elf, Loïk Le Floch-Prigent. The situation was a delicate one. Six months earlier, he had become chairman and managing director of the national rail company SNCF. At the time, the company was still traumatised by the large-scale strikes of December 1995. As far as the judiciary was concerned, his appointment gave him a large measure of protection. The use of coercive measures against him would be a delicate matter, were they to prove necessary. But I could not pretend that the facts did not exist.

The file was getting thicker. I could physically feel the weight of the case on my shoulders. I went to sleep thinking about it; I woke in the morning to find it waiting for me. It was the witching hour. The pressure mounted until it reached such a degree that others could see it. My colleagues told me to be careful; I felt the tension in the financial investigation division growing after some worrying hearings.

I wondered if the sensitive nature of the case was getting to me, together with fatigue. I felt that I was being watched, spied on, and sometimes even followed. I increasingly dreaded my daily trips on the commuter train, especially in the evening. It seemed to me that I regularly ran across people in the carriage who didn't look like normal commuters.

One very warm evening, a man followed me from the platform. He was broad-shouldered, and obviously not one of those dropouts whom one sees sometimes in the suburban trains who stand a bit too close to you: he looked more like a professional sportsman. He looked at me hard. For the first time, I was really afraid. When I got to my station, I got out. He did too. I walked faster. He lengthened his stride, and then abruptly wheeled away.

Over the following days, the locals in my village told us that there had been strange comings and goings of people in cars. Several times the phone rang at home and then hung up as soon as I picked up. I put this down to coincidence but I began to get more nervous despite myself.

The spiral of suspicion is inescapable. I was afraid that they were going to sabotage my car. I asked the owner of a café near the station if I could park it within sight of the café. He promised to keep an eye out. A few days later, he told me that strangers regularly hung around near it. A climate of uncertainty settled in.

On 5th June, neighbours in our little hamlet of about ten houses informed me that three vehicles had taken turns to sit in front of our house, staying put for several hours as if their occupants were waiting for something. I told them that they couldn't stop anyone from walking about, and that they shouldn't worry. The cleaning lady had written down the registration number of one of the vehicles, a light-coloured car, and, just to be safe, I had it checked out.

On 11th June, another car hung around conspicuously outside our house, going slowly back and forth for several hours. A friend was able to take down its registration number and details.[7] I passed this on to the police, who informed me that the registration numbers of that morning's car and that of 5th June were the same. The two differently coloured cars were driving around with the same number plate, evidently a false one.

A show of force

The same day, the assistant prosecutor called me to his office. Although he was as elegant as usual and in control of himself, I noticed that his black eyes were brighter than normal and there was a slight tremor in his voice.

'An old friend asked to see me. I have total confidence in him. He has warned me that you are in danger. Real danger. Imminent.'

'Can you tell me who it is?'

'On the condition that you swear never to repeat it.'

'I swear.'

---

7   It was a dark-coloured Citroën AX.

When I heard the name, I understood that this was serious. The friend of the assistant prosecutor was one of those politicians peculiar to France; partly in the public eye but mostly in the shadows. I could hardly imagine this man, who is used to handling defence secrets, putting about unfounded rumours.

The assistant prosecutor suggested that I ask for police protection.[8] I hesitated. It would be childish to ignore the warning signs: the terrorised witnesses, the dance of the ghostly vehicles, the confidential warnings.

Of course, I know that if a powerful underground organisation with international interests had really decided to wipe me out, they would have endless ways of doing so; all those Italian magistrates, fallen in the course of their struggle against the Mafia despite close protection, were the macabre proof of that. But the police had often assured me that in France, no one placed under their protection had ever come to any harm. We opted for police protection.

I wrote the letter immediately, without including my conversation with my colleague, but mentioning the cars with the false number plates, and concluding as follows: 'Given that these matters are coming to light in a tense atmosphere and while I have several big cases in hand, I think it prudent to ask you for a light protective presence for a few weeks.'[9]

I was living events without taking control of them. This series of events struck me like lightning. I thought that the summer would suffice, and that this decision could dissuade those who were trying to undermine me. However, I was to have police protection for six years.

From the following day, I no longer had any private space. I could go nowhere without a car and two bodyguards at a minimum, sometimes more during critical periods. After a few weeks, the complete list of my friendships was in the hands of the police. No more meetings in cafés. No more window-shopping for pleasure. No more secrets. No more breathing. I lived under the eyes of other people.

At first, the protection was ultra-close, around the clock. The policemen left their guns on the sitting-room table and kept watch in the room next to my bedroom. They picked up the post and inspected each

8   This procedure, particularly cumbersome and costly to the tax payer, mobilises several teams of specialist policemen in rotation. Already used for the protection of anti-terrorist judges, it had never before been put in place for financial judges.
9   Letter to the presiding judge of the Bench, 12th June 1996.

room before I went into it. They asked me to wear a bullet-proof vest. When they walked at my side, they carried a pad of Kevlar in the shape of an attaché case, which was supposed to act as a shield in the case of a possible shooting. It was a demonstration of force which was probably addressed both to those who wished to harm me, and also to myself, as if to make me understand the sensitivity of the situation.

During that same month of June, a witness in the investigation was also threatened and had to be put under police protection. Where did these threats come from? I would never be certain, but I simply had the feeling that I was the object of hostile attention from several directions. This was intensifying but was not yet clear. One's suspicions fall naturally on those people brought in for questioning, whose tranquillity and often impunity were upset by our inquiry. But there were so many of them: managing executives, representatives of foreign countries, competing firms, the secret services...

There were also some units who sought to destabilise my finances, which were made readily available. When I became an investigating magistrate for financial affairs, my husband and I decided that all of our affairs had to be in perfect order, to an almost obsessive degree. There couldn't be a single tax-free consultation at his medical practice, even by mistake. It was a good thing to have done; my life was to be searched, bill by bill. Old friendships would be exhumed. Files would be laboriously compiled and rapidly abandoned for want of concrete evidence. Nobody would have a hold over me. I could be proud of that. But instead, I feel only scorn for these methods which undermined Judge Eric Halphen[10] and for which, in Italy, Antonio Di Pietro paid the price.[11]

At the beginning of July, every level of the judicial hierarchy was on high alert. The date for the summoning of Loïk Le Floch-Prigent to my chambers was drawing near. There were persistent rumours of political intervention. They were all unverifiable and didn't make their way to me. The most nonsensical rumours were circulating. A friend told me that, during a dinner party, he had heard a journalist swear that an emissary had

---

10 French investigating magistrate who led a seven-year investigation into allegations of corruption against President Chirac.
11 In November 1994, Antonio Di Pietro, assistant public prosecutor in Milan and a leading figure in the *Mani Pulite* investigation (of which more later), resigned the magistrature under pressure, after having been the subject of multiple blackmail attempts concerning his private life.

given me 300,000 francs (45,735 euros) in cash to stop my investigations! That seemed so crazy to me that I paid no attention to it.[12]

On 4th July 1996, the hearing of the previous chairman and managing director of Elf, the notification of his indictment and the decision to put him in custody took place in an electric atmosphere which spilled out of my chambers. It was the first peak in the tension of an investigation which would see plenty of others.

Like a red circle

That summer, I learned to live in two worlds: that of the investigation, crisscrossed by turbulence, where words so often had a hidden meaning, where individual interests were advanced under cover of diplomatic interests, where money circulated at the speed of orbiting satellites through a multitude of offshore accounts; and that of my personal life, which seemed to take place on another planet, and which was closer to the life of a French family with no worries in the world.

I did everything I could to make sure that the tempest that I was going through stopped at my garden gate. Unfortunately, life isn't always that simple. Being caught up in the action, I could block out the problem up to a point, but for those around me, the omnipresent police protection made the danger feel very real. The security men and their weapons were a physical incarnation of the sword of Damocles hanging over my head. It was as if I had caught a life-threatening illness; the fear of being contaminated thins out the ranks around you. The fear was like ultrasound, inaudible to human ears, but continually slicing through the air.

It was difficult to carry on as if nothing were the matter. At the slightest incident, the policemen would reach for their guns. One Saturday when I got back to the house, I found the gate to the house half-open. My two travelling companions drew their guns straight away. I only just had time to remember that it was the day for the gardener, and to stop them before they rushed in! Their job was to be on the alert and their tension was

---

12 This farfetched story would resurface during the Elf trial. Between two hearings, off the record, with an air of complete assurance, the lawyer of one of the defendants stated in front of witnesses that he had proof of my corruption, without advancing the smallest tangible proof. The price of my supposed abuse of authority had only been multiplied by one hundred in six years: it was now valued at 4.5 million francs – which at least showed a re-evaluation of my merits.

passed on to me. When we were in the car and they saw a motorbike with someone riding pillion, they reached towards their guns. Opportunity was their worst fear. If they had misinterpreted a situation, the consequences could have been tragic. So I avoided crowded pavements, because a harmless shove might not necessarily be so. I restricted my zone of action.

I played the game by respecting to the letter the security requirements which were imposed on me, in particular the invisible triangle which had to isolate me from others when I was out and about. The men who accompanied me were risking their lives too. Over the course of hours spent in the same car or the same plane, solid links were forged between us, based on small confidences, the sharing of photos of children and memories of journeys. Each crisis was to reinforce our solidarity. I remember one of them, a great hulk of a man, with a view of the world which was entirely opposite to mine, who brought me a bunch of flowers for Mothers' Day, saying, 'I would get myself killed for you...' I was deeply touched, because it was true.

With the passage of time, I have blocked out many of the details of those feverish days, because I just had to get on with my life. For use in this book, I did file away a few personal papers, which cause buried memories to come back to the surface, like this fax, written by a neighbour. I had forgotten it. It is dated 15th September 1996, two months after the imprisonment of the chairman of Elf, and it gives the flavour of those times.

'Yesterday evening, at about a quarter past eight, there was a purple Renault 25 parked about ten metres from your gate. It had tinted windows so I couldn't see the people inside. As I was driving by, this car abruptly drove off very fast. I noticed then that it didn't have any number plates. Driving round the hamlet, down the Rue des Tilleuls, I noticed a dark-coloured Renault 19, also without plates, waiting with its headlights on. The two cars were together. I did a u-turn. The cars had turned into the Rue du Pas-Mauvais, I followed them for 300 metres with my headlights on full beam, to let them know that your property was also under the surveillance of the neighbours. Then I phoned your house to warn you.'

How many episodes like this was I aware of? Ten? Twenty? One day, it was 'friendly advice', another a wooden coffin sent in the post, or yet another witness reporting death threats which made me shiver, despite myself.

Because it was everywhere, the threat ended up being nowhere. I have two hypotheses about this. The first hypothesis is inoffensive enough: rumours have a life of their own, passing from mouth to mouth to return in a loop, nourished by human avidity and, in this case, by the fact that the spectacle of a woman struggling with danger is a captivating one. All those unwitting messengers were just distant flashes from the storm that I was going through.

The second hypothesis is more worrying: the forceful 'advice', midway between a warning and an open threat, was definitely a sign that one does not fight against the higher interests of the country. I realised that we couldn't leave anything to chance. The survival of my investigation depended not just on my bodyguards but also on our ability to stay on the ridge. One false move and we would fall.

When, today, citizens read the proceeding of the Elf Trial hearings, they have a key to understanding the red circle which surrounded me then. In that summer of 1996, I did not know what we were going to uncover, but there were many people who did know the extent of the corruption which had to be protected.

Since the closing of the investigation, I have been struck to learn that many people knew more than I about the level of the surveillance that was focused on me, and the precise nature of the danger that I endured. In a way, I was like an animal caught in the headlights in the middle of the night, seeing nothing apart from a violent beam of light which targets it, and will not let it go.

This threat is almost tangible

Even though, logically, the institution should have closed ranks and protected one of its own who was being threatened in the execution of her duties, at the Palais de Justice, my unusual situation provoked muttering in the corridors and discontented rumblings: 'Look at that circus!' No one had taken the trouble to get my colleagues together to explain to them the reasons for these impositions. The administration is a body indifferent to everything apart from its own peace of mind.

So, fantasy triumphed over reason. What? A low-ranking judge transported all over Paris at the expense of the state, with two giants preceding her into the lift and the office.[13] The bodyguards tried to keep everyone moving in the corridors to prevent a crowd forming. These instructions, which were fundamental to their job, could have been interpreted as arrogance on my part.

Paradoxically, this protection was seen by others as a privilege! I looked like a princess with two servants. All the same, I wouldn't wish that existence on anyone. Daily life turned into a chore, sad and lifeless, lacking spontaneity or anything unplanned.

Some powerful men have a well-regulated life, habitually rushing to the office in the morning at a fixed time, to emerge imperturbably at the same time to the minute in the evening, and they would have worn this noose without thinking about it. I found it terribly crushing. Like all active women, I have a lot going on in my life, juggling separate existences, preoccupied with prosaic tasks. Going into a department store to buy toys for Christmas with two armed policemen is an incongruous exercise that is uncomfortable for everyone, and once you've done it, you promise yourself that you're never going to do it again. Coming back with one's husband from a dinner party with friends on a Sunday evening, as the sun is setting, chatting happily about pleasant things, and two seconds later finding your head thrust to the floor of the car because an alert has been given, spoils more than just the evening.

After several months, I made a formal request that the police surveillance be stopped. This request would be refused. The police management even reinforced its presence by doubling its strength (from two to four policemen) and adding a motor bicycle escort, before later returning to the previous regime. The policemen from the escort would not explain to me the reason for this. These are silent men. This winter, a friend showed me an interview with one of them, written at the time by a journalism student. Once I had read it I was able to understand what these men were feeling. 'Certain threats are very serious; they are not just intimidation. We had learned that a contract had been taken out on the

---

13 An example of these touchy reactions was that of Edith Boizette, head of the investigating magistrates in the financial area, who said in a recent interview with two journalists from *Le Monde*: 'I am not entirely persuaded that three or four years' police protection is truly necessary [...] Deep down, it's all just for show! [...] For [Eva Joly] police protection is part of the external signs of power. [...] It's a benefit that I do not envy her at all. I prefer to go back home in my own little car. [...] We are faced with an examination of the extent of danger, and its real nature.' (*Où vont les juges?* Laurent Greilsamer and Daniel Schneidermann, Fayard, 2002, pp. 54-55).

head of Eva Joly by people who were definitely in a position to pay a killer. This information had been confirmed to us by the intelligence services. Sometimes it feels like I'm in a spy film; this threat is almost tangible. When you begin to get information to the effect that Eva Joly will be brought down unless she eases off, then you begin to get worried. There is a lot of tension around her. When that reaches a certain level, it's very dangerous.'[14] I faced up to the hostile looks of my colleagues in the Palais de Justice because I had no choice. Not a word of sympathy, not even a raising of the eyebrows from magistrates whom I had been working alongside for years. In the corridors, people often showed me a haughty indifference. Inside, I was wounded by this attitude. But I began to realise that this hostility was not directed at me; it was also a way of refusing to accept the reality of the Elf affair.

When justice gets close to the powerful, our internal compasses go crazy; we can easily confuse the fever and its symptoms. It is easier to be scandalised by a possible favour – that the state was providing me with a chauffeur-driven car at the taxpayer's expense, to satisfy the whims of a diva – than to question a democracy in which an inquiry into power and its high priests puts a judge in danger.

This menacing reality sometimes faded away in my mind. I learned to live without thinking about it. But then it would return violently to the fore. Like the high-ranking French general with whole constellations of stars on his epaulettes whom I met by chance at an ambassadorial cocktail party. For a few minutes we made polite conversation. Suddenly he fixed me with his blue gaze, 'I imagine it can't be much fun for you most days, ma'am. The upset, the pressure, the threats… But I think you'll get through it.'

I didn't answer. He paused for a couple of seconds. A grateful smile was forming on my face. And then he spoke again, coldly, 'It would be another matter entirely if you left the world of petrol for that of the arms trade. With us, there's no warning; if you were to begin an inquiry, I'd give you 48 hours.'

His gaze was as cold as his words. He was insistent, as if he were trying to fix his words in my head. I felt as if I had been punched in my stomach, but I made the effort not to totter. And then the conversation took a neutral direction.

---

14   http://www.cfpj.com

From then on, and up until the last day of the investigation, whenever I had to make a difficult decision, this warning would resonate in me, like a thought that you swat away, but that always comes back to haunt you: 'I'd give you 48 hours…'

Happily, I could force myself not to think about the threats every day. One gets used to everything, and the mind ends up ignoring the evidence. A friend once told me about her daily life in Beirut during the war in Lebanon. Horrifying events became so banal that one day she caught herself listening to the radio to find out which way to take to get back from the beach and avoid the mortar fire. With a proper sense of proportion, of course, I have sometimes adopted the same attitude. Each new threat brought the fear back to life, but the other six days of the week, I refused to think about it.

My Ariadne's thread

Our everyday activity was at first a constant struggle against the bureaucracy of the judiciary and the police. The paucity of our resources made our efforts almost derisory. A multinational company like Elf possesses high-tech financial services where highly qualified engineers, pushed by clever commercial lawyers, have, for years, created systems of front companies and secret invisible withdrawals, with branches on several continents.[15] In a list of transactions which could be several metres long, we sometimes had to look for one deposit, which would look just like all the others. We worked 12-hour days, piling up hearings and cross-examinations.

It was amusing to see the surprise of our interviewees when they first set foot in my office, no bigger than a maid's bedroom, having traversed the maze of the galleries of the Palais de Justice, with ceilings five metres high.

These men had not been in an administrative office for ages – unless it was a ministerial office. They wore the Légion d'Honneur on their lapel. Their cufflinks were out of boxes from the Place Vendôme. They had long entries in *Who's Who*. They were keen to show that they were out of place in the rather shabby armchair.

---

15 At that time, Elf had an official presence in one hundred countries, controlled more than 800 subsidiaries and had an interest in 350 firms.

Some simply became confused, and faltered, but the majority could not hide their arrogance. These were cold-blooded creatures, with a sharp intelligence, passing abruptly from a conventional, almost honeyed softness to a curt, implacable tone, full of hatred. They were not used to being contradicted. At their ease in general discussion, they became anxious when faced with prosaic details – which are precisely the things which are most telling. Then, at best, they tried to negotiate, even though we were in the territory of the law and not the contract. At worst, they lost their self-control and confused the Code Pénal with the investigating magistrate charged with its application.

Almost none of them risked admitting that they recognised the evidence, which was sometimes as simple as a suspect deposit of money in their personal bank account. As if the money had been credited without their knowledge and spent by their right hand without connection to the left hemisphere of their brain. I understood, little by little, that they *didn't see* the offences, because they lived in a different physical and mental world.

Despite everything, the investigation advanced in leaps and bounds during that year of 1996. We preferred to concentrate on concrete facts, without seeking to take in the whole picture, at the risk of losing ourselves. As the days went by, our preliminary hearings closed, one after the other. When I had a doubt, it buzzed round endlessly in my head, like a bee against a window. I had to remove obstacles until I understood, and then, when the answer appeared, there were moments of real intellectual happiness.

From then on, I drew a distinction between the balances of power, the alliances, the sensitive zones and the whole sections of the file which had yet to be looked at. The big geopolitical frescoes or the secret business practices of the 'seven sisters' no longer troubled me as much. In this case, personal misappropriations seemed to have reached proportions unknown until this time.

I was holding on to my Ariadne's thread, and I would never let it go.

Under Pressure

At the beginning of 1997, the case got bigger. I already felt like I had lived with it for several years. The pressure around the investigation was mounting. Certain people evidently wanted us to stay where we were. Several witnesses were panicking: I cannot give their names, as that would violate judicial confidentiality. I knew that they had access to restricted information that I didn't have. A female Elf employee, in a strategic post, explained that she possessed such important secrets that she could never reveal them; such was her fear of the consequences, for her and for me.

Another time, a petty thief who had gained possession of important documents, and who had tried to blackmail the circle surrounding one of the people indicted in the case, swore that he had immediately been kidnapped, threatened and beaten up. He gave a detailed description of the office to which he had been taken. He gave by way of corroboration the precise hour and date of a phone call. When this was checked out, it had indeed taken place. The matter would go no further, but it gives an idea of the atmosphere of those nervy days.

Another witness was visibly terrified. He explained to me that, by accident, when they were working on another case, a foreign intelligence service had overheard conversations about him in one of their phone taps. They had contacted him immediately. His shadowy correspondents had warned him solemnly of threats against his life. He had preferred to leave France and did not return for several months. He was convinced that he was going to die, and that I was going to meet the same fate.

The fire

On 4th April 1997 the inquiry called André Tarallo, the managing director
of Elf-Gabon.[1] When I learned about his massive involvement, I issued
him with a subpoena. I cross-examined him. Given the total of the sums
in question, the issue arose of his imprisonment pending trial.[2] The public
prosecutor's office gave me freedom to act as I saw fit. Tarallo's lawyers
argued that he needed to be able to continue his business, in a key post,
at the forefront of diplomacy and business. In this regard, the dates were
unfortunate: he was supposed to be flying out with Phillipe Jaffré, the new
managing director of Elf, for a meeting with the President of Gabon,
Omar Bongo.

Although I was inclined to hold a firm line on this one, I listened to
the arguments of both sides, and withdrew to consider the matter. I could
draw up an order to place him under provisional detention or let the
managing director of Elf-Gabon leave my office without hindrance. It was
after midnight. I weighed up the situation. André Tarallo was no longer a
young man: that very evening, he was supposed to be celebrating his
seventieth birthday. On the other hand, a phone call to Elf's lawyer had
confirmed the reality of the following day's journey to Gabon, and that it
was not an excuse invented for the occasion. I noted that we had taken a
major step forward: an important director of the company had admitted
to possessing a personal bank account in another country. The risks of
pressure on witnesses or of the evidence disappearing were reduced by the
fact of that admission.

I decided to allow Tarallo his freedom and matched my decision with
a record bail figure of several million francs, which reflected the amount
of hidden funds brought to light by the inquiry. At dawn on Saturday, I
returned home with a quiet mind, hoping that I had released some of the
pressure from the case. Instead of facing a wall of hostility made up of

---

1 An alumnus of the École nationale de l'administration, in the Vauban class (like Jacques Chirac),
André Tarallo entered the Entreprise de recherches et d'activités pétrolières (ERAP) in 1967, becoming
administrative director four years later, then geographical director for Africa. He was made managing
director of Elf-Gabon in 1977, a post which he would hold for 20 years. Tarallo would also become
managing director of Elf-Congo (1984), of Elf-Angola (1988), and of Elf-Trading (1992).

2 According to article 144 of the code of penal procedure, provisional detention should occur when
it is the only way to keep evidence intact, to prevent pressure on witnesses or victims, or to prevent undue
consultation between the indicted and their accomplices.

threats and psychological pressure from every direction, I thought that I would be able to set up the inquiry in more normal conditions.

I was completely mistaken.

From the Monday, I saw the tension escalate. At the beginning of the afternoon, I discovered that several passages from the transcripts of Friday's interrogation of various witnesses had been reproduced word for word in *Le Monde*. Such calculated leaks to the press were designed to fan the fire. More seriously, my decision not to incarcerate André Tarallo had immediately been viewed with suspicion. Rumours immediately took hold that I was supposed to have obeyed instructions from the political powers that be: the rumours burned brightly, and were embellished each minute with new details. I was supposed to have received several mysterious phone calls, which had influenced my decision. The story seemed all the more credible because I had effectively changed my mind over the course of the evening. The way I acted, which left a lot of room for contradictory debate, came back to haunt me. It let the idea of secret agreements take hold in people's imaginations.

One of my closest colleagues, who had known me for a long time and saw me every day, looked me in the eye and asked, 'Is it true that Alexandre Benmakhlouf rang you to ask you not to lock up André Tarallo?'[3] I protested and explained matters. On the surface my friend accepted my version of the facts, but in his eyes I could see that doubt lingered.

I learned afterwards that 'well-informed' (but of course anonymous) sources were maintaining that my secret interlocutor was apparently Jacques Chirac in person. Over the course of three days, the rumours had become extraordinary. And yet, I can say without hesitation, that while over seven years I was subjected to numerous pressures, mysterious messengers, threats, anonymous letters, and while I was not always supported by my superiors who were sometimes hostile, the political powers that be never interfered directly in the management of my case. They were too subtle for that – and they have so many other means at their disposal.

---

3   Alexandre Benmakhlouf was at that time Director of Public Prosecutions at the Court of Appeal in Paris. Close to the Gaullists, this magistrate had previously been technical adviser to the cabinet of Jacques Chirac when he was Prime Minister (1986-1988), official representative and then legal advisor for Chirac when he was Mayor of Paris (1988-1991) and again director of the departmental staff of the Justice Minister, Jacques Toubon (1995-1996).

Be that as it may, between the rumours and the truth, the scales were not tipping in my favour. The Elf case was the first to get close to the secret Republic.[4] The sums in question were of a size hitherto unknown in a penal case. The points of reference disappeared, and as always, passion triumphed over fact.

The president of Gabon, Omar Bongo, added fuel to the fire. Under a pseudonym which he apparently used from time to time, I was publicly insulted in *L'Union*, the principal newspaper of his country. He denounced 'the tales of Elf-Loïk-Le-Whatsit-Tarallo-Jaffré and their cod-faced Norwegian bird, Eva Joly... The French are sure to suffer from this latest crisis in Franco-Gabon relations.'[5] Around the same time the press mentioned a tense phone call from Omar Bongo to Jacques Chirac concerning the progress of the inquiry.

The Elf investigation was getting close to the danger zone of international relations, because Gabon is France's private hunting ground. For forty years, close police and defence agreements have grown stronger and stronger. Apart from Elf running their oilfields via offshore platforms in the country's territorial waters, France has acquired a right of priority on the mining of Gabon's uranium, which guarantees the lasting quality of her civil and military nuclear programme and makes it the third atomic power in the world.[6] Françafrique was rumbling.[7] And I thought I'd chosen appeasement!

A fortnight later, early one Monday afternoon, the young police superintendent in charge of the Elf case at the heart of the Brigade Financière[8] (the financial investigation division) sought me out. From the frown of my clerk, Serge Rongère, I saw that something serious was going on. I went over to his desk. Serge brought me up to speed straight away.

---

4   Since Autumn 2000, the affair called Angolagate, investigated by Phillipe Courroye, has revealed other aspects of this part of the shadows in a file, which implicates intermediaries in Angola, Russia and France. According to information which has appeared in the press, the alleged embezzlements are supposed to total more than 150 million euros. The investigating magistrate has also been placed under police protection.
5   *L'Union*, 24th April 1997.
6   The uranium is extracted in Franceville, birthplace of Omar Bongo. The seam is mined by Comuf: Michel Pecqueur, previously high commissioner for atomic energy, predecessor to Loïk Le Floch-Prigent as head of Elf, took over the presidency of Comuf when he left Elf. (cf. *Une guerre*, Dominique Lorentz, Les Arènes, 1997).
7   Used at the beginning of the 1970s in a positive sense by Ivory Coast's then president, Félix Hophuët-Boigny, the expression 'Françafrique' experienced a rebirth at the beginning of the 1990s among the detractors of the French networks in Africa, and the term now covers all the endogamous relationships between France and its former African colonies.
8   British equivalents would be the Serious Fraud Office or the Company Fraud Squad.

'Madame Joly, the sealed packages of evidence from the search of the home of André Tarallo's interior decorator have disappeared.'

The superintendent's voice was extremely tense. I refused to believe it. I was sure that there must have been a mistake. 'Someone's moved them; you'll find them on a shelf somewhere.'

'No, we've checked everywhere. The box isn't there any more.'

I saw red. And I lost my temper.

'That's inconceivable. Empty the dustbins, search the false ceilings, move the desks... You have to find it!'

The theft of pieces of evidence on the police's own territory was an unheard-of event. The building on the Rue des Rentiers was in a total panic. Everyone was aware of the significance of this incident. Luckily we learned quickly that the proceedings would not suffer from it. The policemen had returned from the search in Saint Tropez on the Friday with the documents they had removed. On Saturday, the superintendent was on duty. He had used the time to write up a synopsis of the documents and was able, thankfully, to fax me a copy of the principal pieces of evidence. The housebreaking would therefore not have any direct impact on the investigation.

However, the true significance of this spectacular burglary was to be found elsewhere. If it were not a theft prompted by panic, then perhaps we were facing intimidation. A way of showing dramatically that no institution is safe and that some of our adversaries were at home on police territory. A judicial inquiry was opened immediately, presided over by one of my colleagues.

The following week, we had to go to Normandy and then to Corsica to conduct searches pertaining to different cases being handled through my chambers. We had a series of early morning searches. A search is a marathon, which begins at dawn and often finishes well after dusk. Each detail of the procedure has to be scrupulously examined because the tiniest gap in the sequence of events, such as the overlooking of a simple signature, could result in the annulment of the whole operation. Thanks to the vigilance of our team, in seven years no important search in the Elf case was ever annulled.[9]

---

9   One minor operation alone was annulled by the Court of Criminal Appeal, which considered that we had acted beyond the power of the court.

When we were fastening our seatbelts for the return flight, our police superintendent confided in us. He felt that he was being followed and watched. His words were hesitant; he cleared his throat and spoke under his breath. An oppressive climate had grown up around him, his young wife and their baby. I understood that I was not the only one to live under strain and that we were all in the same dangerous situation, judges and policemen mixed together.

The afternoon of the following day was pure drama. I received a casual call on my mobile phone. The superintendent and his team were among the prime suspects in the case of the missing documents, and had been called in for questioning by the internal police.

As soon as I was warned, I wanted to be there. The principal superintendent of the financial investigation division dissuaded me: in the eyes of the media, my arrival would complicate matters without contributing anything positive. Immediately, I rang the directors of police, and of the internal state security department, and the Director of Public Prosecutions. I explained the situation to them. The policeman had already written up his synopsis, getting rid of the originals afterwards made no sense. I was in no doubt; it was an attempt to intimidate him. I warned those I spoke with that even if a search miraculously found the sealed evidence hidden in his garage, I would not believe in his guilt. And I would let this be known. He was released several hours later, and nothing further came of it.

On the Monday morning, I went to the Brigade Financière in a personal capacity. The tension was palpable. Eyes were lowered, nobody wanted to look at me. I could read incomprehension and hatred on people's faces after that arrest. I spoke to them for three-quarters of an hour. I defended the judge in charge of the inquiry into the theft, who had probably wanted to cover all the bases. But I insisted that I had complete confidence in them. The stealing of the documents was a low trick, carried out by powerful forces who wanted the investigation to fall apart.

The atmosphere changed little by little. Necks unbent. We shared a pizza. Peace returned. A little solemnly, one of them got up and said, 'From now on, we'll concentrate on working for you.' They were won back.

On my return, I learned that the vice-Chancellor, the second in command of our department, was asking for me. With my customary naivety, I thought that he wanted to congratulate me on having re-established contact with the policemen. He greeted me in an unctuous, smothering manner. But he gave me a telling-off, albeit in diplomatic terms. 'Allow me to say that going to the Brigade Financière wasn't one of your better decisions...'

I was shocked by this concern for appearances, which served to appease the judicial top brass to an absurd degree. I remembered a reply from a Viking saga, and very happy to have found the right phrase for the occasion, I answered in the same tone of voice, with a fixed smile, 'If it is the case that one of us is wrong, it's by no means certain that that person is me.' I left his office with a smile on my lips.

In the following days, two years after the beginning of the inquiry, I received several direct death threats. Up to that point I was alone, like a lightning conductor that attracted the bolts. But henceforth, the storm blew inside the institution and attempted to destabilise all our team, even the police officers. On 30th April, I requested assistance in order to share the weight of the case. On 6th May 1997, the vice-Chancellor appointed Laurence Vichnievsky to work alongside me. She was a magistrate ten years younger than me, whom I knew only by sight. Slender, elegant, full of aplomb and with laughing eyes, she radiated energy and self-confidence. She had the tranquillity of 'those who have been born on the right side of life' as Céline puts it.

We were on the same wavelength straight away. In our pairing, she was to be the counterweight and the counterpoint. I appreciated her acute knowledge of the inside workings of the institutions, which would help us in the proceedings. In these troubled times, I felt that two were not too many.

This intuition was borne out by the large-scale search that we organised at Elf's headquarters in the early days of her appointment. This operation marked a turning point. It was a brutal initiation for my colleague and a shift in direction for the case. The oil company, a civil party in the Bidermann part of the case and thereby a victim in the supposed fraud, was connected to it due to the requirements of the inquiry. We followed the money transfer trail as well as various responsibilities. Several directors would have some explaining to do.

Located in the business quarter of the Défense, where skyscrapers from the 1970s and 1980s dominate Paris, Elf's headquarters is a glass building in the form of a quartz crystal, with fifty floors, hundreds of offices, a panoply of lifts and high-tech boardrooms.

Alone, I would have found the search, which was necessary to the investigation, difficult. It was a high-risk operation, in a world of senior executives, where people counted only in millions. The management of a multinational company is accustomed to people bending to its will. Having two of us was a capital asset.

We had prepared our operation with care, poring over a plan of the tower. The crucial thing was to pick the right target and to neutralise, for the period of the search, the offices of the management and the nerve centre of security, to avoid any unwanted escapes. At nine o'clock, we presented ourselves at reception, and in a few minutes, our team had secured the target areas.

Until three o'clock in the morning, that is to say, for more than twenty hours at a stretch, in an atmosphere you could have cut with a knife, we put together more than forty sealed packages of evidence. In the office dealing with security, we found suspect items which did not concern our investigation: extracts from illegal phone-taps, blank special branch-headed notepaper, illegal copies of official transcripts of current judicial investigations, a report on mysterious assassinations in Africa, traces of secret political financing, and so on. We handed these to the prosecutor of Nanterre, who had joined us at the Elf building. As they had been found under his jurisdiction, what was to be done with them would depend on him. I learned afterwards that no preliminary investigation was ever opened.

The evening of that marathon day, of which this investigation would see many, we drove back along the banks of the Seine. We were silent, with the pressure falling away due to the cessation of hostilities. Then Serge, my clerk, who is always imperturbable, meticulously turned out, and whose elegance of dress is reflected in his heart, asked me idly, 'Have you noticed, ma'am, how beautiful the baroque facades are?'

This remark was Serge's way of getting back to grips with reality. It was night-time, but it was impossible for us to sleep. With Laurence Vichnievsky, we decided to stop on the Boulevard Saint-Germain, where a café was still open. To mark this extraordinary situation we shared a glass of rum, drinking a toast to each other.

Between us, as in all human relations, there would be ups and downs, fleeting disagreements and shared victories, but we were never to lose this deep, inexplicable solidarity. In the following pages, I mostly use the first person. I am not empowered to speak for Laurence. But the reader should know that from the day of her appointment to the day of her departure, every decision in the investigation was a joint one.

In the Eye of the Storm

In the autumn of 1997, the inquiry turned its attention to Christine Deviers-Joncour and thereby drew closer to Roland Dumas, France's former foreign minister. He was still one of France's most powerful men.

My personal situation changed. For a few weeks I lived with my son, before moving in, alone, to a two-roomed flat in Paris. When I left his studio flat, at the beginning of December 1997, he was immediately burgled, in a rather acrobatic manner; the intruders made their entrance through a small window situated above a courtyard with sheer vertical walls. They searched everywhere and took nothing: the work of professionals. I felt more than ever under surveillance.

A fortnight later, the flat of Serge Rongère, my assistant, who was on holiday at the time, also received an importunate visit. The burglars came by night over the roof, walking on a gutter twenty metres up. In order to take such risks, they must have been roped up, which indicated training and determination which was hardly compatible with the feeble spoils to be expected from breaking into a studio flat. They also had some nerve; according to a neighbour, the light had stayed on for a considerable part of the night. Obviously, our adversaries were looking for something. A lever for blackmailing the leading figures in the inquiry? Documents that we might have hidden? However, as in Edgar Allan Poe's novella *The Purloined Letter*, there was nothing of that sort to find, apart from evidence of the purity both of our motives and our methods.

On 9th January 1998, after the holidays, we could not get into the investigation chambers. The lock had been forced. Three burglaries in one and a half months. Even without being given to paranoia, I felt that I was

55

now in the eye of the storm, which was hardly the most pleasant sensation I had ever had. I wrote a detailed letter about the incidents, and took precautions; no copy was made of this letter. I requested an audience with one of the highest magistrates in France, the president of the Court of Appeal, and gave him the letter personally. I wanted him to be informed of everything. Just in case.[1]

The impossible secret

We were surrounded by a magnetic field. It was a strange feeling which made me think of the Northern Lights, with their disconcerting colours and the lightning flashes, which cross the sky without any apparent reason. Events were happening faster and faster. On Monday 26th January 1998 at about ten in the morning, Laurence Vichnievsky and I gained possession of important evidence concerning numerous cash remittances to bank accounts belonging to Roland Dumas. Sometimes, during an investigation, certain decisions are difficult to take. Others are more obvious. We didn't hesitate; we had to search the house and office of the former foreign minister in order to trace the origin of these movements, whose size, moreover, had at the time triggered an alert (which had never been followed up) in the section of the bank dealing with money laundering.[2]

Searches are a routine part of the job for a judge. In financial matters, it is less common. Nonetheless, I have never known a search to be useless. When you have a case at your fingertips, the slightest detail takes on an unexpected power. A forgotten post-it leaps out at you, while it's lost all significance for the person who left it lying about. Bank statements, personal archives, memos… everything has a use in the re-creation of the chain of events in a financial offence, which is, of its essence, hard to trace because it's concerned with secret payments and informal agreements.

We all knew, however, that our decision was fraught with consequences.

---

1 At one point, the extension of police protection to Serge Rongère was considered, but nothing came of it.
2 The Maubert branch of Crédit Lyonnais had reported several cash deposits to its parent company. It was not possible to find the file which, according to management at the bank, was destroyed in a fire at head office.

Roland Dumas was the president of the Constitutional Council, the most prestigious institution of the Republic[3]. That does not put him above the law. The same facts, noticed in connection with an ordinary citizen, would bring about the same investigation. But his public position would impose an additional duty of discretion on us. The reputation of the guardian of the constitution would have to be preserved. As is the rule, we had several telephone exchanges with the officers in charge of investigations and members of the public prosecutor's department. The idea was taking shape with them too. We sketched the outline of the operation.

At the beginning of the afternoon something strange happened. Serge Rongère has military training and had, several years previously, worked at the Presidential palace. He is sensitive to matters of security, notably telephone-tapping techniques. Six months earlier, in April 1997, he had taken out a mobile phone contract in the name of a trusted friend who had agreed to be his cover. He had given this name to no one. Serge regularly lent me this secure phone for several confidential calls. Serge's friend has, on her birth certificate, an old-fashioned first name, Josiane, but all her family, her friends and colleagues call her Josie. One day, just after lunch, Serge's mobile rang. A man's voice was at the other end, 'Hello. Can I speak to Josiane?'

Hearing Serge's surprise, the tone of his interlocutor became threatening and the conversation finished with a warning. In our heightened state of watchful tension, when we were obsessed with the confidentiality of the current operation, this provocation shook us. We were playing a game of chess, made up of signs that were indecipherable to those not immersed in the action. This call showed that the invisible eyes and ears had penetrated our protective arrangements. They had acquired total mastery of our communications and wanted us to know it.

At the end of the afternoon, we had finalised our plan. Just before six o'clock, we faxed the representative of the president of the Bar a request for assistance for the following morning.[4] As a precaution, overnight, the order for transport was put under lock and key.

It felt like we were walking over hot coals. The Elf affair was going right into the heart of power. The old police adage came back to me: a

---

3   The nearest equivalent in the British system in terms of prestige might be Lord President of the Council or Lord Privy Seal.
4   This was the due process which had to be followed given the status of Roland Dumas, a barrister.

secret confided is no longer a secret. At least we had limited the spread of the information; two policemen (and their superiors), two magistrates from the public prosecutor's department (and their superiors) and the president of the Paris Bar.

At dawn the following morning, we presented ourselves at Roland Dumas's house. The street was deserted. For a fleeting instant, I hoped that everyone involved had held their tongue. But when he greeted us with a gently apologetic smile and a reproving frown, the president of the Constitutional Council informed us that he had been warned about our search the previous evening, a little before eight o'clock, by a phone call from a journalist, whose name he gave us.[5]

My mind whirled. The law punishes severely any violation of the confidentiality of the investigation. The primary responsibility of every person who has a part in public authority is to protect the inquiry, even if it is directed towards the guardian of the constitution. I did not dare to imagine that anyone in the police, judiciary or barristers had transgressed this. I deduced, therefore, that the telephonic communications from the Palais de Justice were decidedly not secure.

However, as we were there, we had to get on with pursuing our goal. The police did their job without running into any difficulty. The situation became more complicated when we passed to the second stage of the search: the office of Roland Dumas, which was situated at a distance from his home. In two hours our secret had been discovered, and the information had gone round like wildfire: all the exits were blocked by reporters and photographers, who had come running. The close relationship between the journalists who covered general domestic news (news in brief, police, legal matters, etc.) and the prefecture of police must have given rise to an accidental indiscretion, which was then broadcast on

---

5   To be frank, I am not entirely sure that Roland Dumas's informer was a journalist, and I think he had an interest in giving us his name, as a sort of decoy. This seems all the more likely given that in his book *L'Epreuve, les preuves* (Michel Lafon, 2003), the former minister gives a totally different version of this episode: 'I was deeply asleep when the doorbell rang at half past seven. I had no idea of the reason for this call. I hurried to the peephole … and very swiftly got an idea of matters.' Likewise, Roland Dumas reports the testimony of a neighbour, stating that he was awoken by 'a considerable toing and froing of cars well before the arrival of the magistrates and the police. He got up, opened his curtains and looked out of the window to see what was going on. The quayside had literally been invaded!' (pp. 18 and 29) I maintain that the two statements are erroneous: before three witnesses, that morning, Roland Dumas stated that he had been warned about the search the day before. As for the street, it was deserted when we arrived.

the French Press Agency wire from nine in the morning. The alternative was that some people in the know had wanted to stir up the mob to compromise Roland Dumas.

The harm had been done. We had to pursue our task and drive to the minister's office. The only way out was the old carriage entrance. I did not have the police powers to push back the journalists. We had a rapid confab and agreed that we had to confront the hue and cry.

Roland Dumas went first. He chose to get into our car, which was driven by bodyguards. He sat in the middle of the back seat. Laurence Vichnievsky and I sat either side of him. Each of us was trying to put a good face on it. For Roland Dumas, the situation was Kafkaesque. For us, it was uncontrollable. An almost unbearable swirl of flashes blinded us. The photo would be broadcast by the worldwide media and thereafter would often be represented in the headlines as a symbol of high-profile investigations.[6]

For a long time I would reproach myself for that image. At the time, I didn't appreciate the significance of the symbol. The investigation had been caught in a trap. The president of the Constitutional Council would endlessly seek to confound us, his friends adding many rather sexist details, looking to discredit me (I had allegedly gone to the hairdresser beforehand, I had allegedly bought a new suit for the occasion...)[38] That same evening, on television, the Justice Minister, Elisabeth Guigou, deplored the flouting of the presumption of innocence. A shadow hung over our intentions. The focus of suspicion shifted and the polemic ended up covering the real reasons that had led us to search Roland Dumas's house. We did not make the same mistake when we were leaving his office. The way the place was set out lent itself to subterfuge. We climbed a wall and used a second exit, in a parallel street, to get back into the car whilst sheltered from the photographers.

---

6   In his book, Roland Dumas states: 'With the two judges on either side of me I was like a thief between policemen [...] When the judges got into the office car of the Constitutional Council with me (as if I had already been arrested), the flashes went mad [...] The trap had been well set.' (Op. cit., p. 28) I maintain that it was he who chose to get into our car and not Laurence Vichnievsky and I who had imposed ourselves on that of the Constitutional Council – the photos are proof of that. Between the two versions, there are several shades of meaning, from the banal truth – an unexpected and unpleasant situation which each of us was trying to face up to – to some imagined machination.

38   'I find it hard to believe that there was no premeditation. That multitude of journalists gave the impression that someone had stirred up the paparazzi. The objective was not discretion, but rather publicity. Who could profit from this set-up? Who constantly sought out press attention? Who took pleasure in posing for the photographers?' Roland Dumas, op. cit., p. 29.

The inordinate media coverage of this search made us feel vulnerable. Up to then, despite inaccuracies and exaggerations, and apart from the *ad hominem* aggressiveness of the *Nouvel Observateur*,[7] the media had given wide but serious coverage to the Elf case. It was a time of scandals. The case was the latest episode in the long and saddening tale where French society discovered the criminality of its elite. The real surprise came from the sums of money involved, which necessitated extra zeros all round.

But all this collapsed in January 1998. We felt an ill wind blowing. Targeting a high-level politician who was the moral authority of the Republic led to media frenzy. Things were spiraling out of control. When a case achieves a certain degree of notoriety, it becomes a victim of the 'curse of the cuttings file', and articles on it become compilations, where truth and errors become mixed up and form a separate story, a kind of soap opera of true lies. Media truth fed on itself, and risked supplanting the reality of the case.

'Who killed Eva Joly?'

The whirlwind did not abate with the end of the search. The following morning, the computer of the principal officer in charge of investigations for the Elf case showed clear signs of having been hacked into: his hard disk had been read. The principal superintendent of the financial division told me that he had received a phone call from a journalist with *Le Monde* who had been told of the incident. The press knew about an IT theft in the financial division almost in real time – or, in any case, before I did.

There was always a message to decode. All our deeds and gestures were observed, or even anticipated. The slightest piece of information was passed on to the press, who were only too happy to get these unattributable scoops. But the real intention of the leaks was not to influence public opinion. The shadowy informers were instead seeking to show us that nothing that happened to us was unknown to them, and that they had the upper hand. That evening, a thought ran through my mind

---

7   The star investigative journalist of the weekly magazine, *Airy Routier*, had made the former CEO of Elf into a cause célèbre. According to his own account, he was contacted at the beginning of the affair by the lobbyist Olivier Le Picard, who worked for Loïk Le Floch-Prigent and introduced him to his lawyers. So I became the target of the magazine, which was, besides, historically close to Roland Dumas.

whilst I was going home. In this game of cat and mouse, the roles had been reversed. I was now the mouse.

The whole area had become ultra-sensitive. From now on, I had the feeling that at the slightest action, a journalistic ball of fire would surround us and that we would be swept away. I have lost count of the number of times I heard, during the course of our investigation, the expression, 'That will open Pandora's Box!' It was as if, in order to make progress, there was an entrance ticket, a price to pay in the direction of the truth, at almost every step.

Because danger could come from anywhere, it made us mistrust any external intrusion. I got into the habit of keeping a sort of logbook, to keep a trace of the sequence of events. If we spoke on the telephone it was in hints or acronyms that had to be decoded. The hours before and after each important hearing were tension-filled, for fear of a leak or of intimidation.

There was no let-up in the threats. The day after a search in the offices of a lawyer, the clerk found my desk lamp knocked over and unscrewed and the phone socket clearly pulled out. As with the theft of the sealed evidence at the financial division, it was about showing us that no sanctuary existed and that my chambers were open to every passing burglar.[8] Later on, the key to my apartment turned in a void: the lock had once again been forced. With each incident I had the fleeting impression of being the prey in the hands of an invisible predator.

Ethologists have discovered that when the nervous systems of chimpanzees are repeatedly submitted to electric shocks, they get used to it. Over the course of time, the strength of the shock has to be increased to cause a reaction of the same size. At the end of several weeks, the hardened animal can cope with a shock which would have killed it on the first day. When life pushes you like this, each burst of adrenaline harms you and immunises you at the same time.

The only antidotes I had were pride and action. I became used to fear. I lived with it like one struggles with a shameful illness. But it is not a noble feeling. It makes you sweaty and dull. Sometimes, when the strain was at its height, I got up in the middle of the night. I had bad dreams. I often dreamed that I was being pursued; I took shelter in a lift-cage and

---

8   An inquiry into these events would be expedited, without success.

knocked at every floor. Then the doors would shut, or else I could hear frightening breathing. I had a recurring nightmare: I saw one of the bodyguards level and aim his gun at me. I used to wake up with a start. I left my bedroom and slept on a sofa, on the opposite side of the dividing wall from where the policemen were keeping watch.

I learned to live with these anxieties. I knew that I had to hold on tight, without letting myself be overtaken by the pressure which could affect my judgement. I had to keep reminding myself that I was doing my job. Just my job.

Out of propriety, the members of our investigative team never spoke to each other about these troubling moments. But I am sure that in an unconscious manner, they welded our team together. The friendship which had grown up between Laurence Vichnievsky and me, the generosity of the representatives of the law who, week after week, piled on long days for no extra pay, consistent confidence in the police from the financial division, or in our colleagues in the public prosecutor's department, made a sort of human current which made light of the danger. Unfortunately, this did not reach the floors which separated us from the those higher up the ladder. The enthusiasm of the early months, when we were a team in the front line of sensitive investigations, was forgotten. The hindrances we endured turned against us.

Roland Dumas's implication was like a shockwave whose resonance increases with time. His friendships and allegiances of many kinds, his familiarity with the Palais de Justice since the 1950s, his apprenticeship in the Cabinet with the then Justice Minister, Elisabeth Guigou, and with a good number of ministers of the Jospin government, his warm relationship with the President of the Republic, Jacques Chirac, his prestigious public function, keystone of the arch of the constitution; it was all in league against us. According to a rule as old as the administration, the solidarity of the institution stops where its tranquillity begins. We were henceforth a thorn in the sides of the vice-Chancellor of Paris and the Director of Public Prosecutions. The investigation put them in an awkward position in the natural order of things, because they had to take on an inquiry which provoked the hostility of the authorities upon which they depended. A crack was inevitable. Imperceptibly, our team detached itself from the judicial mainstream like an iceberg separates from the glacial ice-cap.

The reactions of those around us during stressful times were generally warm. They oscillated between fear (which keeps you at a distance) and light-heartedness (which makes you clumsy). So it was with a colleague who gradually became a friend. She and her husband had me over regularly. They enveloped me warmly in their friendship. One evening, her husband had a mysterious and playful air. I knew him to be a part-time writer who worked occasionally at a publishing house. He wanted to show me his most recent project, a thriller mystery for which he already had a title: *Who Killed Eva Joly?* Obviously, he had no idea of the effect that this sentence would have on me. I was mute with indignation. 'It'll be funny,' he assured me. Obviously I no longer had a sense of humour.

Interference

In spring 1998, a fresh incident made us certain that our telephone lines were being tampered with. One morning, the superintendent of the financial division spoke to us to alert us to a new development. For several hours, he had tried in vain to fax us an urgent document of several pages. The communication got lost on the way in a fashion that seemed strange to him. In fact, two offices down, the fax got through fine.

From then on, we began to monitor the fax machine: it sometimes took a quarter of an hour to receive a document. When we moved the machine to another phone line, it worked correctly. But in our office, it was a very capricious creature. We called a technician to back us up. After checking, he assured us that our equipment was in perfect condition, apart from 'an interference problem'. He added on his service report: 'Sensitive site, check the line'.

Our incident report to the president of the tribunal met with the same irritated silence as the preceding ones; just another piece of paper to put in the shredder. No one saw fit to check anything out. One could well ask oneself who, in the Elf case, would have an interest in creating 'interference' on our line and who would have the means to do it? Since the beginning of this investigation, surely we were living in the best of all possible worlds, surrounded by people due to be tried who were respectful of the law, in the calm of an uncomplicated inquiry?

The telephone soon became a means for summary communication, used only for inconsequential exchanges. Instead of being an ally, it was an encumbrance. Listening devices today are of a sophistication that makes James Bond's instruments look like old-fashioned antiquities.

Laurence Vichnievsky and I rapidly got used to the idea that when the need made itself felt, a few well-placed men could follow our work at will.

The definitive proof of this came in March 1998, during the interrogation of André Tarallo. Suddenly, Laurence Vichnievsky burst into my office and dragged me outside, which never happens during such important procedures. She took me to her chambers and passed me the phone, with the presiding judge of the court of criminal appeal on the line. A quarter of an hour earlier, she had tried to ring me. My phone had not rung, but she had instead been surprised to listen in live to the hearing of Andre Tarallo, the CEO of Elf-Gabon, taking place in the next room.

My telephone had become a concealed microphone, usable simply by dialling my internal phone number. I drew up a statement on the incident for my superiors. Straight away, the rumour went round the building that I had become paranoid and given to mythomania. 'It's her delusions of grandeur!' I noticed knowing smiles, faces ostentatiously turned away at my approach. The rumour grew rapidly, and came back to me in waves throughout the following day. It was necessary for the presiding judge of the court of criminal appeal to go to the head presiding judge of the Court of Appeal to testify to the truth of the matter.

That was how it was sometimes; passing our time proving that we weren't crazy, whilst such grave violations of the law – such as recording the contents of an interrogation, or listening in to a magistrate – only drove us to further action, without troubling anyone at the heart of the judicial hierarchy.

We lived in a strange society, where such extraordinary practices as the thefts of sealed packages of evidence, unauthorised phone-tapping, tailing and dirty tricks had almost become ordinary to us. Who makes a fuss about these things any more in France? For ten years, in the cases which I have been in charge of, or partially involved with, the destruction of archives has appeared to be the national sport. I have experienced in succession the arson attack which set fire to the warehouses in Le Havre which housed the Crédit Lyonnais archives; the unexplained fire which devastated the head office of the same bank; the equally mysterious destruction of the archives of a sister company of Crédit Lyonnais on the eve of my visit; the disappearance of a case of sealed evidence in the offices of the financial division; the burglary at the office of FIBA, the Franco-

Gabon bank, on the day after a search, to clean out the drawers just in case I would have wanted to come back and have another go... Not to mention the shredders going at full pelt through whole sackfuls of paper in the hours preceding our arrival.

I'll stop there. Such a depressing list of offences makes the Republic of France look like a sham democracy where criminals have the arrogance of impunity. Organised networks built on sophisticated logistics, permit themselves everything: harassment of magistrates, theft of statements, burglary of any home, or destruction of compromising pieces of evidence. But the world turns upside down: the suspects seem protected, whilst one mistrusts the magistrates.

Not to lose face

Seen from the inside, the apathy of the judicial administration in the Elf case was impressive. The word 'security' was unknown to them. Our telephone lines were unchecked. Computers were vulnerable. Our offices were not protected. Our superiors swanned about in an unreal world, acting as if a unit under orders from a former president of the Republic had not been caught *in flagrante delicto* carrying out unauthorised phone-tapping,[1] as if the great armaments and oil companies did not have intelligence units which sometimes acted violently, and as if the networks of influence of all varieties were not insidiously operating at all levels of the establishment.

Outside the anti-terrorist zone, magistrates are supposed to manage alone, faced with harassment and intimidation, whether they are inquiring into the burglary of a jeweller's or are in charge of a case such as ours, dealing with the embezzlement of several billion francs, and subjected to pressure emanating from the high level management of France and abroad.

I obtained an additional lock for my office at the Palais de Justice – a derisory seawall made of sand in the face of the mounting waters – and

---

1 Opened in March 1993, the investigation into the Elysée taps had brought to light the hidden actions of the 'anti-terrorist cell' created in 1982 by François Mitterand, which had at its disposal, without any real control, 20 discretionary tapping lines. Dozens of people, including lawyers and journalists, were spied on for more than ten years on the orders of the head of state. In August 2002, Judge Jean-Paul Valat sent 12 people – including several prominent politicians – before a criminal court for infringing individuals' right to privacy.

we decided, with Serge and the assistant who supported us, to take it in turns to do the cleaning. I bought a vacuum cleaner and in the evenings we were transformed into housekeepers, to avoid unwelcome visits masquerading as cleaning. Up until the day I discovered that through carelessness, a copy of our key labelled as belonging to our office had been left hanging on a board in a secretary's office, open to everyone.

The incident reports which I filled in were also lost in the shredders. I sometimes felt like one of the characters in the film *Brazil*, bombarding their superiors with abstruse correspondence, which flies out of their offices at the slightest breeze. Disconnected from reality, part of the judicial hierarchy put their energy into not losing face. It was touched with Chernobyl syndrome. The important thing was not to respond to the event but to preserve the institution.[2] Appearances had to be kept up, the air sweet, the armchairs comfortable and the ushers obedient. To admit that we were vulnerable and under attack, in the heart of the Palais de Justice, was the sole unpardonable crime.

An arrest warrant lost in the sands

Our inquiry was viewed by the public powers as an excrescence on the system, which in no way concerned them. So, when I discovered the constitutive elements of a case of fiscal fraud, I sent the file to the services concerned, as I am obliged to. In the Elf case, the sums involved were considerable; millions of francs in cash that had not been declared, payments to Swiss bank accounts, and so on. I was to learn later that certain cases, which were nonetheless the most significant breach of public trust, involving several million francs, were treated *a minima*, or even with manifest indulgence. This was to me a clear signal that those in power protect their own.

Likewise, another scandal cast a shadow over the law. On 5th January 1999, *Le Monde* revealed that the international arrest warrant issued for

---

2   In September 1986, the French government, supported by a battery of experts from the Commission for Atomic Energy, stated that the radioactive plume from Chernobyl had missed France, despite the contamination of Belgium, Germany, Switzerland and Italy: the wind had mysteriously respected international frontiers. Subsequent measurements contradicted this assertion, but back then it was more important, in the eyes of the administration, to protect the image of the atomic industry than to keep French citizens informed.

Alfred Sirven, one of the principal suspects in the case, only covered Europe.[3] For nearly two years the warrant had only been effective within the limits of the Schengen Agreement, plus Switzerland; a serious anomaly. The paper's journalist had discovered this secret through tenacity and a series of coincidences.

We moved heaven and earth to find out what had happened. I had indeed drawn up an international arrest warrant and passed it to the public prosecutor's office – which is responsible for its distribution – for execution. But the link seemed to have failed; the section of the police designated to ensure its transmission across the world had lacked zeal, I was told. It's hard not to see the close relationship of the suspect with the secret services as an obstacle to the proper functioning of justice.

However, it was we who carried the public responsibility for it. The chattering classes who pull strings, dine with royalty and hide themselves all over the city had already accused us of calculating behaviour and making underhand agreements and alliances. This attack would bear fruit. A large part of public opinion assimilated the idea that we had not even looked for the key witness in our case.

---

3   In its editorial, the paper accused us of 'an incomprehensible lack of zeal which discredits the investigation of the Elf affair, damages its rigour and undermines its coherence.' (*Le Monde*, 6th January 1999).

A revolver

Spring 1999. 6 o'clock in the morning. A wet, grey Parisian drizzle was falling. The previous evening I had warned my bodyguards that we would be leaving early. I hadn't given any more details. When you are planning to search someone in police circles, it's better to be discreet. Laurence, Serge and I had already worked out the route. The suburbs of Paris are sometimes a sinister maze, where motorway slip roads, concrete barriers and random buildings, warehouses, houses, bits of wasteland and hypermarkets are intermingled.

We were acting with as much care as if we were attacking a terrorist cell. Seen from outside, the infinite precautions that we had taken over the preceding days, our concern that morning and the silence weighing heavily in the car must have seemed incongruous. The service record of the man whom we were investigating was rather thin; he was a modest retired police official.

But his reputation was as great as his discretion. We had merely to write on the official form the goal of our little jaunt ('the dwelling of Daniel Léandri and all other relevant places discovered in the course of the inquiry') for some nebulous disquiet to make itself felt from the policemen who were accompanying us.[1]

The French police organisation is an extraordinary one. Since the revolution of 1789, France has had plenty of civil wars. The police have

---

1   During his court appearance in connection with the Elf trial, Daniel Léandri presented himself as a simple guardian of the peace, originally 'seconded from the Ministry of the Interior to follow francophone African affairs, then official representative during the periods from 1986-1988 and 1993-1995' under the orders of Charles Pasqua. He was one of the closest associates and the favourite envoy of the chairman of the RPF.

always found themselves at the epicentre of these political upheavals. In each war that pitted Frenchman against Frenchman, particularly under the occupation and during the Algerian war, the police have been subjected to infiltration and dirty tricks; they have seen whole strata of secret networks laid down, and then disappear from view without ever disappearing entirely.

Out of habit, the parties of government let personal networks develop with branches in Corsica, the Middle East, Africa and in numerous large public companies. These networks of secret fidelity and proximity, where appointments are a subtle game which would not look out of place in the Soviet-era administration, and where it is the done thing to speak amongst each other in Corsican, weave a spider's web in the minds of many policemen, feeding paranoia in some of them.

Everyone in police headquarters felt watched by someone and they proceeded, like Norwegian islanders walking on thin ice during the thaw, in the hope that the ground would not collapse beneath their feet.

We arrived at Léandri's official address, a small unaffected suburban house. His wife opened the door to us. Our man was absent. It was obvious that the house had only had someone in it for a couple of hours. It was very cold. A recently unpacked suitcase was open on the floor. The fridge was empty. There were spiders' webs on the lampshades. Once again, the leaks had preceded us. Our visit had become public knowledge and the retired policeman's modest house had been reoccupied in a hurry.

The householder was not there, but he had left something for us. A little personal touch. On the empty table in the sitting-room, in the open, was his Smith & Wesson revolver. The gun was pointing at the door. I recoiled. The provocation was obviously also intended for the inspectors of the Brigade Financière who dared to lend a helping hand to investigations of the French police's forbidden city; the networks. The revolver was loaded.

Unknown at this address

Unflustered, our little team got to work. I confiscated business cards and bank statements and checked the telephone. During searches I always take with me a briefcase containing a portable fax. I was therefore able to send letters rogatory[2] to the nearest police station from a country home or a secluded pied-à-terre whose existence might be discovered in the course of the investigation (which was to be the case that day).

Three hours later we set off towards Daniel Léandri's office; he had kept a foothold in part of the police administration.[3] We asked to speak to his secretary. She said that she was surprised that Mr. Léandri was not there. The previous evening, on leaving, he had said to her, 'see you tomorrow,' as he usually did. But he still had not turned up, even though he had two meetings in the diary.

The phone rang. As is the rule, Laurence Vichnievsky answered in the place of the secretary and heard one of the journalists who was covering the Elf affair. He was ringing to find out what was happening, thinking that our man would answer. Laurence caught him off guard.

While this was going on, I looked at the diary. I discovered a visitor whose name was familiar; it was the man in charge of police protection who was responsible for, among others, my security. I could have found more reassuring information. I also stripped out the list of calls received; by worrying coincidence, several of Daniel Léandri's old colleagues who were high up in the organisation had tried to get hold of him towards the end of the previous day.

There was no question of relaxing our grip, despite the intimidation of the revolver. A sign had been addressed to us and in the language of power, it was a direct threat. We had to react with another symbol, which would mark our determination and prevent the escalation of tension. It was a dialogue at a distance.

We immediately branched off to the Council of the Hauts-de-Seine Département where Léandri also had a base, according to a business card seized at his house. The building was deserted, almost ghostly. It seemed to us like it had been emptied of its occupants. Or perhaps it was a trick. From the office boy to the bored receptionist, we ran up against a blank wall. The man did not have an office here, he was not known at this address.

---

2   A letter rogatory is a formal request from a court in one country to 'the appropriate judicial authorities' in another country requesting compulsion of testimony or documentary or other evidence or effect service of process.

3   The SCTIP, Service de cooperation technique internationale de la police, whose mission, according to the internal police regulations, is to 'co-ordinate the organisation and functioning of the police abroad: training or technical advice for non-EC countries, gathering of intelligence with reference to the internal security of France, promotion of French industry in the area of security equipment, etc.'

I persisted. We got out his business card; it carried a phone number and we compared it with the internal list. It came up trumps. It was the number of the personal secretarial staff of the chair of the Council, Charles Pasqua[4]. We went there. On the record of calls, I again found several messages intended for Léandri, but no trace of his presence. The man was a shadow.

Thus it was for our inquiry; a universe where the reality of power is not to be found in offices or in the official organisational diagrams. This is a world where titles have nothing to do with what the individual is actually doing. This power has its own geography, its own codes, its own networks, its own methods. And manifestly, it does not wish to give an account of itself to the law.

No inquiry was to be launched into this peaceable retired citizen, not even for having kept a police revolver after having left the police service. The protection from which Daniel Léandri benefited would allow him to escape from disciplinary sanction, even though his official office space was quietly taken away. He himself was to explain that he had simply 'forgotten' about his revolver when he left.

The police officer from the Brigade Financière in charge of the investigation and a partner in this episode felt resentment from colleagues in the police force for having dared to violate the sanctuary of the networks. A few months later, as he was leaving his office, a man with a strong Corsican accent threatened him directly. The man was just a messenger. But the words which he had been charged to pass on weighed heavily.

---

4   French Minister of the Interior (1993 - 1995) and Chairman of the Union of Europe of the Nations (UEN) group (1999 - present).

Manipulations

At the beginning of 1999, the inquiry was finished or, at least, the parameters of the case would move no further. We had sized up the Elf galaxy. The embezzlement of several billion francs had been discovered, as had the greater part of the hidden networks. In Geneva, our colleague Paul Perraudin was doing the groundwork, bit by bit, on the jumble of accounts about which we had asked for further information; we just had to wait for the results of his painstaking work. Additionally, in 14 months we had investigated the section on abuse of company funds in the Dumas / Deviers-Joncour affair. The machine was set in motion and it seemed like nothing could stop it. Nothing apart from a serious setback.

After three years of direct intimidation in which the 'forgotten' revolver on the table marked a pause, those who did not wish our investigation to reach its conclusion decided suddenly to change tactics. They had probably realised that the strategy of placing us under physical tension had failed. Despite their threats, we had not given any ground on our determination to investigate. But there was another area over which we had no control; that of public opinion and the networks of influence. They now set to work on this. The pressure shifted up a gear in a few weeks.

It all started on 26th January 1999, with a ordinary search of the office of Maître Eric Turcon, a former tax inspector who had become a fiscal lawyer and who, at one point, had had Alfred Sirven as a client. The lawyer protested forcefully against our intrusion. In the hours which followed, he expanded on this by inventing imaginary exchanges, saying that I had rummaged in his secretary's handbag and that I had impounded his computer – both entirely false. This sort of behaviour no longer worried me and passed over me like water off a duck's back. After two days of fiery communications, everything calmed down.

On 17th March, the Dumas affair took off again. We had to re-open the investigation, which had been closed since December 1998, because of new charges brought against Roland Dumas.[1] Faced with the media tumult which accompanied the revelation that his mistress had used Elf's money to pay for antique statuettes bought for him at auction, Roland Dumas decided to 'retire' from the Constitutional Council.

Immediately, behind the scenes, forces got moving. Underground alliances were forged. And, as if by magic, a fortnight later the Turcon affair suddenly resurfaced. On 1st April 1999, in a terse announcement, the Council of the Order of Lawyers at the Bar in Paris announced its intention to sue Laurence Vichnievsky and me for violation of professional confidentiality and the rights of the defence. It was a stab in the back.

For a magistrate, there is no more serious accusation than that of bias or violation of the rights of the defence. When the charge comes from the order of lawyers, it becomes an exceptional event. From such a point, the recusal of the investigating magistrate by the president of the court 'for the serenity of justice' becomes possible, even if the magistrate has done nothing wrong.

The attack was unjust, but the shot was well-aimed. In its presentation of the facts, the allegation purposely used the confusion between the status of fiscal lawyer – which would confer no immunity – and that of defence lawyer, protected by the law from any investigation linked to his client. The solemn tone reinforced the idea that we had committed a serious act.

The first head in the trap

I felt as if I had been done a great injustice. Until the Elf affair, I had always maintained excellent relations with the lawyers 'under the faith of the Palais' as tradition has it, the word 'faith' being understood in the sense of 'confidence'. The smooth progress of investigations requires a certain

---

1   Christine Deviers-Joncour having insisted on bringing new elements in her possession to the knowledge of the law.

understanding. Everyone plays their role, but the rules of the game have to be common to all. I had always kept my word with the lawyers. Before each decision, I really examined cases from all angles in order to listen to the arguments of every party.

But the Elf file was so enormous that it required the involvement of more than 80 lawyers, the cream of penal business law. These multiple relationships demanded sensitive handling. The infernal media interest in the affair, which unsettled all our personal relationships, had created an environment conducive to emotional outbursts.

In this instance, it seemed rather convenient that the code of ethics accorded so well with the interests of Roland Dumas's lawyer, ex-president of the Bar and member of the office of the Council of the Order of Lawyers which, as if by coincidence, had just demanded our recusal on grounds of bias.

I got lost in conjecture. At root, I was sure of my good understanding of the law; the jurisprudence of the final court of appeal is constant, and that search had been legal. Two representatives of the president of the Bar were present that day and they had noted nothing abnormal.[2] My certainty blinded me, and I was going to be the first to put my head into the trap that was held out to me.

The very next day, I met up with some journalists from the foreign press and had a casual conversation with them. Although up to that point I had limited my public contributions to two or three interviews on the means allocated to the law, I had also regularly accepted private invitations to speak about institutional matters, because I think it is important to exchange points of view with society and not to stay locked up in a bubble.

That morning I was trying to make my listeners understand that financial crime does not just concern the mafia, casinos or nightclubs. Financial crime nourishes an immense grey economy whose beneficiaries present a perfectly honourable façade. I drew on the work of several experts, notably in the area of the laundering of drug money,[3] which showed that a considerable part of the benefits of this trafficking accrued to several affluent respectable foreign lawyers, who helped establish front

---

2   Besides, effectively becoming a lawyer in the case in 2001, at the return of Alfred Sirven, Eric Turcon would not demand the annulment of this search by the Court of Criminal Appeal.

3   cf., for example, Jean de Maillard, *Un monde sans loi*, Stock, 1998.

companies, gave advice on tax optimisation and contributed their procedural knowledge.

I used an unfortunate phrase: 'There wouldn't be any money laundering without lawyers. Fifteen per cent of criminal turnover goes to the lawyers.' The generalisation – *the* lawyers – was a stupid thing to say. If my mind had not been occupied with the action of the Council of the Order, I would probably not have used lawyers as an example, but bankers, which amounts to the same thing. My subconscious was doing the talking. I spoke that sentence, which was buried in a conversation of almost two hours. Then I went back to my office without thinking any more of it.

When earth decomposes in autumn, it flourishes; mushrooms grow in a few hours. Before noon that day, an agency dispatch which took my declaration out of context, unleashed an impressive tempest. Within a few minutes, Serge Rongère was weighed down with faxes and requests for interviews, whilst the indignant communications to the French Press Association piled up.

Some colleagues put their heads round the door of my office, distressed. In these sorts of cases, the logic of the media system is infernal. The Elf affair had become a soap opera. If nothing happened, attention dropped off. So the media invented new developments, following the old principle of Pierre Lazareff: 'One piece of news plus a denial equals two pieces of news…'

Had the avalanche started off by itself? Had someone made the most of my slip by stirring things up behind the scenes? The fact remains that Resistance, Honour and Principles, all the capital letters in the dictionary of the Rights of Man, were invoked against me.[4] If I had struck a prisoner I would have had less opprobrium directed at me. The Justice Minister denounced the 'offensive and regrettable statement'. Roland Dumas's lawyer thundered against a 'banana republic'. The President of the Conference of the Bar spoke, quite seriously, of 'the risk of slipping by stealth towards totalitarianism …'

The most unreal assailants and coteries fell over each other to attack us. On 6th April, Eric Turcon's lawyers submitted a direct citation against

---

4   Like the headline in the *Nouvel Observateur* of 14th April 1999, 'Feu sur Eva Joly', ('Eva Joly Under Fire').

Laurence Vichnievsky and me for 'violating the home', 'violating the right to private correspondence' and 'obstruction to the execution of justice'. On 7th April, the Council of the Bar requested that the Justice Minister refer the matter to the CSM (French state body that appoints members of the judiciary) to sanction me for what I had said, since it 'revealed an absence of impartiality which is by its nature incompatible with the exercise of jurisdictional functions'. The demand for recusal was not explicit, but thinly veiled. The Council of the Bar appointed Henri Leclerc, a former president of the League of Human Rights, to represent it in its complaint covering the search of Maître Turcon's office.[5] Laurence Vichnievsky was reluctantly caught up in the tumult. 'Of course, Eva, you will contradict what you said.'

'I can't do that. I said that sentence. It is taken out of context but I said it. There were 30 witnesses. I do not want to lie and make out that they twisted my words. I have to take it on the chin.'

It was then that I understood the extent of my colleague's solidarity in bad times. I had entrapped myself through my temperament. Laurence could have broken away, and shielded herself in high principle, to the applause of the Palais de Justice. With a good dose of calculation and a touch of cynicism, she could have got back sole mastery of the investigation, as the authorities would probably have been delighted to use a possible disagreement between us in her favour. But she chose to close ranks. Although this effort cost her, she even agreed to help me draw up a diplomatically-worded letter of explanation to the Council of the Bar, which, supported by conciliatory steps from several high magistrates, reduced the tension.[6]

We had a long-standing agreement that the following weekend we would give ourselves three days' rest in a mountain chalet lent by a friend. Laurence had bronchitis and a temperature of 39 degrees and her husband had to stay in Paris, but she refused to cancel. She drove 900 kilometres

---

5   The Order called into question the responsibility of the State which is, in the terms of article 781-1 of the Code of Judicial Organisation, 'held to repair the damage caused by defective functioning of justice' following 'irregularities observed during the search' (*La gazette du Palais*, 4th April 1999).

6   The magistrates' unions rose up against the Bar's steps which, according to them, 'sought to prevent the pursuit of investigations which implicate the highest personalities of the state, notably the president of the Constitutional Council.' The complaint was finally withdrawn and the Justice Minister did not refer the matter to the CSM. Maître Turcon would go as far as appeal, but his proceedings would not reach a conclusion. They finally died out on 14th February 2001.

with me, rather than see a rumour of discord spread in the Palais de Justice. Despite my mistake, she stood shoulder to shoulder with me.

Don't go near the windows

This inordinate volley of verbal violence showed that, as far as the media were concerned, the Elf affair had reached a point of no return. The disproportionate coverage of the inquiry rendered the slightest of our declarations explosive and the smallest of our acts uncontrollable. This state of affairs was the goal sought by those who had endlessly informed the media before a search, who transmitted statements at strategic moments and in short, dragged the affair into a vertiginous spiral. All the precautions that we had taken to protect judicial confidentiality had not prevented this tidal wave. Our investigation had become the pretext for a widespread denunciation of every 'show trial'.

I understood that the violence would take place henceforth on the media's territory, where, as I was sworn to silence, I could neither reply nor counter-attack. The impotence undermined me.

In such a sensitive inquiry, an understanding of the situation is a capital asset. Danger gives one a sixth sense. Anyone who has been in an exceptional situation will understand this. It is inexplicable. Several times, when the strain diminished, I noticed that I had known what to say and had done what had to be done on a sudden intuition or impulse. But now, it was the opposite.

These attacks affected and wounded me probably more than all the death threats to which I had been subjected because I could do nothing other than watch my public trial, mute and shackled. The Italian judges had also experienced the wake of the *Mani Pulite* investigation: a progressive slide where the judge sees his credit undermined in public opinion, day after day, by unpleasant insinuations, total fabrications, or overt accusations of criminal behaviour. This Chinese water torture is then finished off by a recusal on a trumped-up charge of bias.[7]

---

7   One of my former colleagues, Armand Riberolles, analysed the situation thus:'A school of thought is in the process of being born, a new defence called 'rupture' which consists of playing the judge rather than the case. It is obvious that Phillipe Courroye or Eva Joly have been on the receiving end of this new 'rupture' defence where one attacks the judge.' (In *Où vont les juges?* op. cit., p. 148).

80

In the secrecy of the institution, the psychological pressures reached a new level. One morning, I was summoned to see the chief presiding judge of the Appeal Court, an extremely rare privilege for a simple judge. We were in his monumental office, one of the most prestigious in Paris. The air was muffled, softened by beautifully bound books and Gobelins tapestries. I seated myself in an institutional armchair and had to listen to what he called a 'simple piece of advice from a friend'. 'I have it from an extremely reliable source that you have now entered into an extremely dangerous area. Do not go near the windows...' I started, flabbergasted.

'Be on your guard, all the time and everywhere. It's very serious.'

I was to be told no more. He assured me of his support. I thanked him and went back to my chambers, taken aback and feeling powerless.[8] I was profoundly upset to hear this sort of talk from a man who had always defended magistrates who had been endangered and unjustly attacked.

I was caught between fear and incomprehension. The meeting left me with a nasty taste in my mouth. The benevolence of my interlocutor was obvious; he was under no obligation to let me in on this secret, and his doing so was a mark of confidence. Perhaps he was even taking a risk as far as his 'informers' were concerned.

Even so, I could not prevent myself from thinking that we were in a decidedly strange country. One of the highest magistrates learns that a judge is in 'extreme danger'. When? From whom? How? Had he passed on his concerns to the Justice Minister or the Ministry of the Interior? We would never know. On the contrary and with the best intentions in the world, he had called in the target and passed on to her the kind of 'advice' that had been heard so many times in Palermo or Bogotá, in the shadow of the mafia: 'Do not go near the windows...' When the only latitude given to the highest judicial authorities is that of confidentially warning magistrates of the danger they are running, the invisible part of the Republic has decidedly gained a great deal of ground.

A fortnight later, when the media storm of the Turcon affair was unleashed, when Roland Dumas's lawyer denounced a banana republic, no authority took the trouble to support us, even in private, nor to

---

8   Soon after our conversation, on 12th March 1999, the chief presiding judge of the Appeal Court issued an order for close protection with regard to Laurence Vichnievsky, who up until then had been spared threats.

underline that the real banana republic is perhaps where an investigative magistrate avoids working with her back to the window for fear of being shot.

This conversation illustrates the two dimensions in which we had to go about our business. To all appearances, French institutions seem solid, and they are often shown as an example to foreign countries. We live under the rule of law. But *at the same time*, I had to carry out my duty as a magistrate in an oppressive atmosphere, flanked by bodyguards.

The ambivalence of my situation also applied to Elf, which had over the years stood out as a high-level firm to the point of becoming the number one national company. The façade was prestigious and the firm seemed to be performing to a high standard. But *at the same time*, we were discovering embezzlements sometimes totalling almost hundreds of billions of francs, adding up to nearly a year's profit. Did all industrial scandals have a double bottom in the no-man's-land of financial globalisation? These questions would continue to occupy my mind over the years, without my ever being able to supply a definitive answer.

Confronted with the reign of impunity, with the inversion of the usual relationship between corruption and respect for the law, we constantly had to rethink our vision of the world. It was a perpetual revolution. Yesterday's truth no longer coincided with what we were discovering. And we knew already that tomorrow's truth would surpass today's understanding. The investigation which we were undertaking was, in a true sense, an investigation of ourselves; we were discovering another order of things, behind the façade.

Directly from the Minister

Outside the Palais de Justice, the media coverage was getting more and more surreal. Facts became diluted in anecdote. After a year of the 'Dumas affair', between 'whore of the Republic' and gifts to lovers, the Elf case had become a banal pantomime in the eyes of the public. The gap was growing between the reality of the stakes in the investigation and the media representation of those involved in it.

The consequences of this complete inversion of values were quick to makes themselves felt. The most persistent – and unjust – rumour would have us responsible for violating the confidentiality of the investigation. At the beginning, I could shrug off these rumours. However, I became alarmed when I realised that these accusations were being made by the highest political and moral authorities.

During a meeting granted to us by Pierre Truche, a prestigious magistrate, counsel for the prosecution at the trial of Klaus Barbie, I noticed that he quite clearly turned his back on me and only spoke to Laurence.

I was astonished by this. The great mind answered me icily, without using the usual polite 'Madame' of French speech, 'I have it directly from the minister that you are the source of the leaks in your case.' I felt as if I had been punched in the solar plexus; I was appalled. And I replied in the same manner. 'I have the advantage over you of knowing that that is false. I am sad to learn that the minister has been manipulated.'

Our hostile exchange demonstrated the demonising of my public image. One of my magistrate friends told me indignantly about having heard the prosecutor of a large court in the Paris suburbs swear in front of witnesses that after each interrogation I used to fax the transcript over to *Le Monde*! Simple common sense would have sufficed to destroy this accusation, leaving aside the risk of blackmail which would come from the sending of a single judicial document on headed paper showing my chambers' fax number... But I was able to explain, to those who would listen, that the telephone lines were manifestly under surveillance. I was also permanently accompanied by two policemen who had to do a daily report on my movements to their superiors; the police being what they are, I imagine that my diary was then passed to the Ministry of the Interior. Is it possible to believe for a second that during six years I could have been stupid enough to violate the confidentiality of the investigation within the sight and hearing of the French authorities, whilst everyone was watching out for the smallest false step and whilst I was within sight and earshot of all those who wanted my ruin?

Nonetheless, it was enough to ask ten people at random in the street to realise that the popularisation of scandals in the media was primarily attributed to the magistrates, who were the only silent people in the whole circus. The same myths, repeated over and over again, had ended up taking on a life of their own. 'Three hundred and seventy lies make a truth,' wrote Huxley in *Brave New World*. I have no illusions. One person cannot turn back a tidal wave. All I can do is to tell the truth and hope for the best.

Everyone knows it but few people say it. Rare are those who write it, especially among the magistrates. But everyone agrees in private that the violation of the confidentiality of the investigation is sometimes a police or political practice – an opportune leak at the highest level of the organisation – but almost always it is the fruit of an association between a journalist and a lawyer on the case. I write these lines tensing my fingers on the computer, for fear of being on the receiving end of a bolt of lightning from the Bar for slander and attacking the divine right of the defence, or of provoking an immediate complaint from the League for Human Rights to the European Court of Justice for having advocated a return to the worst times of barbarism and totalitarianism. But I'm just stating something that is common knowledge, which is not contested by any investigative journalist worth the name.

Connections operate in every sensitive investigation. In exchange for access to certain pieces of evidence, journalists give the complicit lawyer access to their computer at an opportune moment, or relay arguments which serve their client. These links with the media are all to the benefit of the lawyer; it helps him in his strategy, maintains his reputation and, indirectly, keeps everybody in business. The press, for its part, gets in return first-hand information which it publishes with the seal of authenticity conferred by an official inquiry. The practice is so widespread that, from case to case, friendships are forged, and the old habits resurface almost automatically.

I imagine equally that this complicity could be coupled with, in certain limited cases, some dishonourable behaviour and a monetary exchange of some sort. After the closure of the investigation, I met a great French intellectual and renowned essayist, who admitted to me that he had been approached several years beforehand to say good things about Elf for money. For this one who refused, how many accepted? Hundreds of millions of francs in cash have circulated in this affair, smuggled in suitcases directly from Switzerland. The press cannot have been the sole power to have escaped corruption, even if the idea remains taboo.[9]

With each party unveiling the evidence which is most favourable to their defence, certain shadowy zones remain carefully sheltered from public

---

9   A great Spanish journalist, Juan Tomáás de Salas, former editor of *Diario 16*, testifies to the same drifting in Spain: 'Ideals have vanished. There is no investigative journalism, only secret powers that often filter information in its guise. These powers have used us in their personal battles.' (*El País*, 22nd July 1994).

curiosity, because it suits nobody that they be revealed. In a paradoxical way, the confidentiality of the investigation in the Elf affair had probably covered numerous elements of the case which would have been interesting for the public. As I had an overview of the whole of the evidence, I amused myself one day by doing a little calculation on a blank piece of paper. The result was edifying. Two thirds of the file had escaped the interest of the media, which had all too often concentrated on the gossipy elements.

Show trials

On another level emotions ran high, which entailed that everything was permitted, and the principal people indicted didn't put a foot wrong. Detention on remand or an indictment is a social stain. The only way to compensate for the damage was to transform the accused into a victim, albeit in a symbolic sense. The greater the social status, the more dazzling the search for compensation. Every week offered us a new exclusive with shocking testimony, with blaring headlines and featuring barely readable facsimiles, all of which continued to serve up the same indigestible brew. At the risk of aggravating my case, I can say with certainty that the lawyers who were the most eloquent at denouncing this spiral were often the same ones that kept it going.

The tearful testimonies in the papers were a heady mix: conditions in prison, which are always good for some column inches; the fall of a man, always saddening; and the inquiry, nevertheless described as necessary. It is the symptom of a reversal of values. To focus on the suffering of a deposed man is to leave aside the debate.

In principle, I don't blame the press. That would be too easy. Its interest is legitimate. The notion of the confidentiality of the investigation was initially conceived to protect the inquiry and not the indicted. There are countries where the charges which weigh on an indicted person are clearly exposed in the course of certain 'windows' in the procedure, without it constituting an attack on human rights. On certain subjects of general interest – and the presumed embezzlement of several billions of francs at the heart of a public company is one of them – freedom of information and democracy should require that inquiries be transparent. While most of the politicians and intellectuals raised a hue and cry against the judges, some courageous journalists could be found defending the application of the law to the powerful. They were, however, few indeed.

But in the absence of clear rules, the worst and the best became confused: gratuitous accusations, false information, artificial fits of anger, human interest stories were all mixed up with that of the scandal. From my ivory tower, I gave up trying to understand the logic of the press. During a search, for example, we found traces of payments by dubious establishments of considerable sums in cash to certain prominent journalists, such as a particular editor, or an alleged expert in terrorism. The evidence had been placed on the file. I imagined *Le Canard enchaîné*[10] having a good laugh about this corruption of minds. But nothing filtered through and the silence has lasted until today.

On the other hand, the press could make a headline out of something that seemed minor. One day I was questioning the managing director of a foreign sister company of Elf. In the course of this interrogation, he let slip, almost in passing, a few accusatory words about a firm belonging to the former Prime Minister Edith Cresson. The hearing finished late at night. No copy of the transcript was made. Serge Rongère placed the original in the safe to which he alone had the combination.

Just after lunch the following day, *Le Monde* published as its top story, with a full inside page, large extracts from the transcript. I thought that this document was securely behind a thick layer of metal, but the essence of it was in the paper. Either hidden microphones had allowed outside ears to follow the interrogation and to organise an opportune leak, or the IT network in the Palais de Justice was leaky and the hard disk of the clerk's computer had been scanned, or one of the protagonists of this hearing had left his mobile phone on or had recorded the interrogation. In any case, the harm was done. The paper went to press at 11 o'clock. But the article also featured numerous supplementary elements of which I had not had any knowledge.

In this case, it was me that they were looking to manipulate. The 'spontaneous' outburst in my office the previous evening was a deliberate strategy. Supported by a press operation – a supporting dossier passed to a journalist who hadn't asked for it – it sought to orient the inquiry in a devilish direction, probably to incite a counter attack.

---

10   A French satirical magazine.

In a case as complex as this one, with so much at stake, the inanity of confidentiality of the investigation was obvious. The law is powerless in an epoch that is dominated by the media. It professes a dogma which nobody respects any more apart from the magistrates. And yet they are made the scapegoats for the phenomenon of 'show trials'. The injustice is striking. It is impossible to open a specialist pamphlet without seeing the little ritual paragraph concerning 'the inopportune and scandalous revelations orchestrated by certain magistrates' who, 'unaccustomed to the spotlight, have given in to the lure of stardom.'[11] It's stunning, but it's true.

---

11 *Décideurs juridiques et financiers*, no. 41, p. 61.

An Untenable Position

In the summer of 1999 I went on holiday in a state of fatigue such as I had never known. The media frenzy added stress to our days. We didn't spend hours discussing claims made by one or the other. It was simply another issue to deal with during the coffee break. When I had to prepare my defence against Maître Turcon, I had to use a weekend night to respond to the twenty-eight points of his complaint, such was the pressure on my time. Faced with an uphill battle against all sorts of perils, we had to work twice as hard. There was no other way to complete the necessary investigations successfully.

The scale of the affair created an additional responsibility. Each affirmation required ten verifications. The twists and turns of bank accounts, from Vaduz to Geneva, the offshore firms, transfers of money in London... all of it had to be understood and retraced. The interrogations sometimes went on until midnight. I spent evenings alone at home going through documents with a fine-toothed comb, tallying things up, underlining contradictions. Often I prepared for hearings by setting the alarm clock for 4 a.m. In a few months, I put on five kilos, as if to compensate for the accumulating tension.

The key to several mysteries was to be found abroad. We waited with impatience for results from our counterparts in Switzerland and Liechtenstein. However, the judicial system of the banking havens regurgitated appeal processes, even appeals against appeals, whose only effect was to hold up the transmission of documents. We knew in advance that the foreign pieces of evidence would not be put on the file before 2001 at best. The appeals in Geneva gave 18 months' respite to those who wanted to prevent the investigation from coming to its conclusion. Those under investigation knew the importance of time as well as those investigating them. These months of waiting seemed interminable to us already.

The case had become an octopus, which occupied whole shelves of the library. The traps and manipulations could make us stumble at every point. In proceedings like the Elf ones, involving chambers of hardened lawyers, each judicial act is sifted and dissected. Professionals are paid to uncover faults in the argument and to exploit any openings for an appeal. It's the rule of the game. Whole sections of the investigation are contested, sometimes several times, before the Court of Criminal Appeal – and up to the final Court of Appeal. By the end, the investigation would have been validated ten times, which constitutes a sort of record.

The autumn of 1999 was a busy one, without a moment's respite. At the Palais de Justice the looks were getting more and more hostile. The press campaigns had left indelible marks. Laurence Vichnievsky told me several times that she wanted to change jobs. Two years of pressure, with their share of anonymous phone calls, threats, weeks without getting your head outside, bodyguards... It was a heavy price to pay. In her book, she says, 'I began to run out of energy. And I felt that I was nearing a state of mental and physical exhaustion.'[1]

For my part, I felt that I was at a crossroads. These four and a half years under high pressure had given birth to a double of myself, made up of bits and pieces, which had escaped me. The fact of risking one's life causes uncontrollable reactions which differ from person to person, depending on how one copes with danger. Buried in our subconscious, this preoccupation is an ancient one. Emotions range from rejection to envy, admiration to scorn, and reason cannot control these passions.

Despite myself, I had become a figure upon whom people's anxiety was projected.

For those holding management positions, I was the lightning conductor for their fear. The image of power and business depicted in the Elf affair was a reality they refused to confront. Friends told me of wild talk. Men and women gifted with reason, with an IQ above the average, were behaving like pedlars at a fair. They painted a picture of a former Trotskyite open to all alliances (this allegation about my alleged

1 Laurence Vichnievsky (with Jacques Follorou), *Sans instructions*, Stock, 2002.

membership of a clandestine organisation had the additional benefit of being impossible to disprove), a CIA sleeper charged with a mission of destruction against the jewel of the French petroleum world (another lie that was all the more credible for being unverifiable), a manipulator with an unquenchable thirst for social revenge, without faith or law, a megalomaniac drunk on fame, using totalitarian methods...

The worst thing was the gullibility of these city dinner circles, where a well-placed word was enough to start these seemingly indestructible rumours. Thus it came about that I had been a militant on the extreme left in my youth, a rumour that has never faded away and which would resurface from time to time like my own personal Loch Ness monster.

No human being can remain impervious to the picture that people paint of him, especially when it is such a caricature. In the mornings I looked at myself in the mirror without blushing. I haven't stolen so much as a stamp in my life. I lived in sixty square metres on thirty thousand francs a month. My whole life testifies to the fact that I have honourable motives.

I knew too that a large part of the population supported our investigation. The positive figure of the judge, wife and mother who is taking on the men of power has a strong magnetism, even if it is just as fanciful as that of 'that woman from the north who has come to destroy French industry'. France is a country of invisible castes. My Norwegian origins made it impossible to define my place on the social chessboard. I was 'the foreigner' and that was put to my credit. Without knowing much about our action, the people made us carry the considerable weight of their frustration with all injustices.

It seemed to me that these two currents, which were converging towards me, were combining dangerously with each other. Soon I would no longer be my own property and the situation would become genuinely uncontrollable – at the risk of hampering the investigation.

To make the lines move

For the Christmas holidays I decided to spend a week in Tunisia. On the plane that was to take my old friend Tone and I there, we chatted about unimportant, happy things, like two college girls who had just bumped into each other. The plane prepared to take off, but came to a sudden halt at the end of the runway.

Cars with wailing sirens and flashing lights were coming towards us. The door opened and policemen in combat gear rushed down the central aisle. They literally picked me up and dragged me with them, half-carrying me. I was extracted at a run from the plane, head lowered, leaving the other passengers dumbfounded and frightened. The security services had become involved because of a bomb alert. I heard fragments of explanation in the confusion: 'assassination attempt', 'bomb', 'target'. I repeated inwardly, 'they wanted to kill me, they wanted to kill me...' Luckily, it was a false alarm. Nonetheless, a little later, in a customs office in Roissy, I had a nervous reaction to the shock and trembled uncontrollably.

I understood that we could not hold on much longer without moving the lines. Our position was no longer bearable. With Laurence Vichnievsky in agreement, I started the search for another magistrate capable of supporting our efforts, even possibly taking up the baton if one of us decided to fold our hand or if the manipulators managed to get us taken off the case.

For several months I put all my efforts into getting Renaud Van Ruymbeke to join us. He had many positive attributes. He had run several investigations into party political finances showing great resolve and independence; this experience and impartiality were indispensable for our multi-layered case. In addition, he was, together with the prosecutor Bernard Bertossa, one of the first signatories of the Geneva Appeal.[2] This would be an advantage at a point where a significant part of the case was being played out in Switzerland and we had to collaborate closely with our foreign colleagues. And moreover, he was a man, a fact that could reduce to negligible the more male chauvinistic attacks on our inquiry.

Renaud wasn't sure he wanted to leave Brittany. Tall, with tousled hair, always a little stiff, but sometimes voluble and almost childlike, he had an engaging personality. He finally decided and we sealed our alliance. However, the Justice Minister didn't view it in that way. For several months, the promotions list of the Brigade Financière was frozen by her office so that an objection could be made to his candidacy. But Renaud

---

2   Launched by seven European magistrates on 1st October 1996 at the University of Geneva, this appeal for the free circulation of preliminary inquiries was signed by more than 4,000 of their peers.

Van Ruymbeke was the oldest candidate at the highest grade; political will could do nothing against that. He joined us in April 2000. Straight away, I decided to delegate whole sections of the case to him.

When I came back from the Christmas holidays, I made another important decision: to speak openly. I wanted to destroy that image which allowed the media harassment and psychodramas, like the experience with the Bar, to happen. I have always thought that free speech, if it is accurate and authentic, can undo a crisis.

I received several offers from publishers, some of which represented disproportionate amounts (including an advance of up to 150,000 euros). I chose a young independent house that had been in existence for less than a year, and I opted for a trifling advance. I was looking to be heard, not to line my pockets. The director of éditions des Arènes, Laurent Beccaria, had been one of the organisers of the Geneva Appeal, together with the journalist Denis Robert and the publisher of *Un monde sans loi* by Jean de Maillard, a reference book on financial crime. There was a feeling of mutual trust. He knew that we were on a knife edge and that I could sink the entire Elf investigation with one word too many.

And so in the evenings and at weekends I very quickly wrote a first book with him, half autobiography, half essay.[3] Since I was still on the case, I knew that defiance was dangerous. I hesitated over whether to publish the book. According to the terms of the contract I could stop the publication right up to the last minute, all the more so since the book had taken a more personal turn than I had envisaged at the beginning. Could a magistrate who had been criticised (wrongly, in my view) for the excessive media coverage of her case decently publish a book which would reinforce her notoriety and the suspicions about her wish for publicity? But the situation was exceptional: since I had become a public figure and French society had placed me at the centre of the story, the better it was that my voice be real and not artificial.

It was a game of poker, played out on the margins of the case. If things turned out badly, I could lose everything and discredit our work. But at least I would fall having tried to make myself understood. On the other hand, if I succeeded in setting my truth against the fantasy, we would win ourselves some breathing space. When I signed off the proofs, I cleared my

---

3   *Notre affaire à tous*, Les Arènes, 2000.

Eva Joly

mind. I weighed up my decision and accepted that by publishing this book I could be dismissed from the case. Nevertheless, I was convinced that I could not do otherwise. Fortunately, people listened.

The media greeted this book with a mixture of astonishment and benevolence.[4] As my interlocutors would often say to me, 'so, after all, you're not as bad as all that...' I received thousands of letters from both anonymous people and influential magistrates. All of a sudden, the noose loosened.

For some weeks, the case went through a calm period, as if the truth had attenuated the violence that we were facing and dissipated misunderstandings. In September, the Bar invited me to a reception, which I attended. The president of the Bar took my arm and greeted me warmly, as if we were old comrades. I said to myself that the 'surreptitious totalitarian threat' must have dissipated during the summer... In the depths of my conscience, where one's self-esteem is found, I was profoundly soothed by it all.

A flaw

In the autumn of 2000, there was the beginning of friction in our team. Behind the battling and energetic qualities of Renaud Van Ruymbeke, who was capable of putting in hours of work without losing his fierce concentration, we discovered a magistrate who was a stickler for seniority. Although he was happy to put in long days and finish the case on time, he did not want to encumber himself with consultation or with drawing on our experience of the case. So the collaboration between Renaud and Laurence was difficult. These two strong characters struck sparks off each other. We had several arguments which resolved nothing. We therefore split up the files, with clear boundaries between each, which did not

---

4   In *La face cachée du* Monde (Mille et une nuits, 2003), Pierre Péan and Phillipe Cohen alleged that the decision of *Le Monde* to publish extracts from *Notre affaire à tous* was by way of thanks for the information which I was supposed to have passed to the paper, of which I was, according to them, an 'honourable correspondent'. I have never passed the smallest piece of information to Hervé Gattegno, the journalist assigned to the Elf case during the investigation. I once telephoned the director of the editorial staff of *Le Monde*, after the publication by the paper of the provocative article on the extent of the arrest warrant for Alfred Sirven, in order to set the record straight about responsibilities within the justice system. The person with whom I spoke took note of this. The pre-publication agreement was in fact negotiated between my publisher and Eric Fottorino, the editor-in-chief of the centre pages of *Le Monde*, without my being there. I obviously issued a writ for defamation against Pierre Péan and Phillipe Cohen.

94

correspond to the transparent and clear way in which Laurence and I had worked up to that point, but which meant we could progress together.

I appreciated Renaud's contribution, because Laurence was slowing down and I was getting tired. I had absolute confidence in his independence. His firm character was an insurance policy against any pressure. But for all that, I refused to do what he suggested one morning in a Montparnasse café; change the order of nominations and let him manage the case. Confident in his qualities and his masculine drive, Renaud could imagine no rank other than the first. I knew that the case would be in good hands if it fell to him. But if I compared his six-month sprint with the number of pages which attested to my work since 1994, I did not see sufficient reason to let myself be supplanted on a case of which I had the most thorough knowledge.

Happily, we succeeded in keeping these disagreements over precedence from prying eyes. From the outside, the ranks were united, as indeed we were united on what really mattered. There were 60 high-level lawyers and dozens of journalists waiting to pounce. The change in confidence was like a hidden flaw in a piece of ore, which was invisible to the eye, but which made the stone fragile. Luckily, it would never collapse. At least not publicly.

The appeals, which had been multiplying, were extinguished one by one. For those indicted the closure date of the case was drawing inexorably closer. The incidents during the interrogations became more frequent. The electricity was palpable. Certain people openly shunned me and launched charm offensives on Renaud. I found this little game, which contributed nothing to their defence, puerile. By banking on my fall they would not change the flow of money nor the charges which weighed on them. Whatever my future, the case would not change.

But in their eyes I had become a paroxysm-inducing figure, a voodoo doll who warded off fate. The screen of protection afforded by my book was dissipating day by day. Serge Rongère observed the situation with his habitual detachment, suffused with melancholy lucidity: 'We shan't manage another year like this, ma'am.'

A Fortnight

The Vietnamese have a saying that a simple leaf, however small, contains a whole tree; like a miniature, the veins sketch out a trunk, branches and the roots. The first fortnight of February 2001, which was extremely violent, was a miniature of the Elf affair as I knew it.

As far as the Alfred Sirven trial is concerned, I cannot reveal the inner workings of the inquiry without breaching my professional confidentiality obligations. Each section of this story is a novel in itself. Our efforts lasted months, and featured dead ends, rumours, contradictory depositions and police informers. It led us to Africa, to the Middle East and finally to the Philippines. For hundreds of hours, often despairing of success, we checked out the smallest lead and pulled every string at our disposal.

In the Philippines the battle was a sensitive one. The local police received several death threats. Two of their informers, moreover, paid a heavy price: one was shot in the neck, the other knocked over by a car. Both were seriously wounded. A Filipino investigator passing through Paris expressed fears for his safety. At our request, a permanent team of French policemen was dispatched there.

In this mission to the far corners of the earth, for the first and probably the only time, we could count on the complete support of the French authorities. The first section of the Elf trial had begun without Alfred Sirven, who was one of its principal suspects. The closing of the main investigation was drawing near. It would be impossible to bring to judgement the largest financial case ever investigated in France in the absence of one of the three principals indicted: Sirven had fled, stating that he had 'enough material to blow up the Republic twenty times over'.

On Friday 2nd February 2001, a little before nine o'clock, the police who had been dispatched to Asia rang to tell us that Alfred Sirven had been arrested. Laurence was at the airport, leaving for Palermo, and her mobile phone was on voicemail. As at the end of every week, Renaud was getting ready to join his family in Rennes. After a quick conversation, we agreed that there was no point in both of us staying, so I remained alone at the controls to sort out the considerable legal and diplomatic shambles that was the return of Sirven to France. At the outset, the authorities suggested sending a military aircraft to Manila. But each hour counted. Our representatives on the other side of the world feared that there would be subterfuge, as Filipino justice has not escaped the venality and corruption that has contaminated the country for decades. From one hour to the next, the extradition warrant could be contested by time-wasting methods. Launching interminable and uncertain proceedings in Manila was a risk that we could not take.

The first available commercial flight for Europe was a Lufthansa one. I opted for this solution. The airline and the local authorities agreed to delay it so that the prisoner and the policemen could make it. At the stopover at Frankfurt, a straightforward transfer was planned, but a German judge requested an opportunity to cross-examine Sirven in connection with the inquiry into the secret financing of the Christian Democrats. A fresh imbroglio. Hanging on the phone for a twenty-hour stretch, I worked with the French authorities to find a solution.

Two days later, Alfred Sirven landed in Paris with his escort.

I shall always remember the times when I continually had to make really difficult choices. I suddenly rediscovered the joy of collaborating with other public agencies, like at the beginning of the Elf affair when we formed a united team with my colleagues in the public prosecutor's office. Things were like they were before the soap opera began, before I was demonised for having got too close to the heart of power – something that bites and burns.

This arrest was a collective success for the legal institution. Nonetheless, the judicial timetable posed a procedural problem. The trial on the first section of the Elf affair was under way. Alfred Sirven was involved both with these hearings and with our further investigations, which complicated the situation. At the request of Claude Noquet, the chief vice-president of the court, who watched over the course of the trial, a meeting of more than 20 people was organised in a packed public prosecutor's office. We decided to notify Sirven of the charges brought against him on the very evening of his arrival in Paris, leaving the following day entirely free for the hearing. We wanted to avoid the spectacle of a jammed courtroom waiting for Sirven for hours, if he decided to make the suspense last and prolong indefinitely his stay in our chambers. We did not want to risk invalidating the detention warrant.[1]

Over the following days, I felt as if I were going through a hall of mirrors in a fairground. Had the crazy media attention on the Elf affair thrown the legal machine into disarray? As though filtered through an invisible prism, all the events of that week took on enormous and grotesque proportions. The prefect of police blocked off half of Paris to prevent any getaway attempts during Sirven's transportation – reinforcing his notoriety and the farcical aspect of his arrest. In the Brigade Financière, despite the late hour of his arrival, his appearance in my office dragged out since I had to read him a litany of several dozen charges.[2] He was visibly tired by his trip. Then it was Laurence Vichnievsky's turn, and finally that of Renaud van Ruymbeke, a little after midnight. The following day, the press accused us of cruelty for having overwhelmed the man by night. Human rights issues were once again invoked. 'The three judges in the Elf affair fought over an old man. Eva Joly made our client undergo inhuman treatment,' thundered his lawyers.

The world was crazy. Here was a man suspected of the embezzlement of more than a billion francs and who had lived on the run for several years. And in one fell swoop, his arrest, expulsion and court appearance were presented as the return of the Spanish Inquisition! I had come to the realisation that words no longer made any sense. The only things that remained were pretentious boasting and verbal bidding wars.

The abscess threatens to explode

Two days later I received a bilious letter from the presiding judge of the court. He began by saying that, henceforth, he forbade night-time court appearances, as though I, personally, had made a mistake. He probably did not know that this solution had been proposed by his services and that we had accepted it out of solidarity with the institution.

---

1   A warrant for arrest only provides for 24 hours' detention. A decision to place the arrested person in custody must be taken before the expiry of this period, or else he or she will be automatically freed.
2   Having taken account of his age, we had arranged for medical supervision, which had prolonged his presence on our premises all the more.

The judge then went on to express surprise that I had given champagne to the Filipino investigator. This man had arrived at Roissy airport in deepest winter in sandals, and no one had thought about him. He had not slept in a bed since the previous Friday. I had organised a get-together in his honour with the French investigators, who had done a magnificent job. That seemed perfectly legitimate to me. I knew what this investigation, from its very beginning, owed to personal chemistry. If each of us had done our conscientious and obedient government-service jobs without using our personal initiative, the Elf affair would have remained the Bidermann affair, probably closed by a decision that there was no case to answer right after it had been opened.

However, in the twisted and deformed reflection of the time, this spur-of-the-moment get-together became an affair of state and an indication of bias. The legend of an investigating magistrate celebrating the arrest of an indicted man with champagne was born. It lent weight to the idea that the drunkenness of fame had made me lose all sense of proportion.

I always made the mistake of wanting to sort out what wasn't working. I like things to move. But by doing this, I had put myself in the firing line. With all the media attention on the Elf affair, I should have retreated into the ranks, put on the appearance of a little grey mouse, become silent, predictable, acquiescing to all the absurdities of the French judicial administration, which is so creative in these matters. I had made the mistake of continuing to be myself.

There's a saying that the venom is in the tail. The president concluded his missive with a lapidary and threatening phrase: 'I learn with sadness of the dissension at the heart of your team.' He asked me to account for it. I took this letter for what it was: a call to order. The conclusion of the inquiry on the trail of Alfred Sirven, who represented the key piece of the puzzle we had put together over long years, would not be our Everest. While we could be proud of the work done, it now appeared to be a time for ill will. The fall was close: I was a dead man walking. I felt as if I were radioactive, and contaminated everything I touched.

I concluded that the ripples of our periodic differences with Renaud Van Ruymbeke on such and such a point of procedure had leaked despite our efforts. A point of steel had buried itself in the wood of our team and was trying to break it at the joints. When I suggested to Renaud that he meet the presiding judge with me, he refused, saying, 'I would have too many things to say...' I tried to speak to calm the situation, but he dug his heels in. The abscess was threatening to burst without my really knowing why it had got to such a point, or what was going to make it burst.

For the good of the trial's progress, I gave eight weeks' respite to Sirven, without removing him from his cell, so that he could prepare his defence before the criminal court. Although Laurence had no objection to this decision, Renaud obstinately refused to accept it. We argued about it one evening, on the pavement outside the restaurant where we had just had dinner with our opposite number in Geneva, Paul Perraudin, and the Swiss experts accompanying him.

Renaud stuck with his position. 'I am going to summon Sirven. It's absurd to let things drag on. We've already waited too long. We are two investigating magistrates. We have the same rights. Eva, you know I am free to do it.'

'It's impossible. I have given my word. Legally you are not linked to me, but morally you are. I am the judge in charge of the principal case. I asked you to join us. I forbid you.'

That was probably one sentence too many. The following day, my husband died.

Chaos theory has it that a simple flutter of a butterfly's wing in Guyana unleashes a typhoon in Sri Lanka. In the same way, in our lives, certain events follow on from one another, sometimes in a diabolical fashion, devastating all on their way.

I left my job for three weeks. On the day before the burial, I received a call from the principal superintendent of the Brigade Financière, Noël Robin, with his team in the background: 'Madam, I wanted to let you know that I have just refused to carry out the letters rogatory by which Mr. Van Ruymbeke asked me to remove Alfred Sirven from his cell. This is the first time in my career that I haven't carried out a judge's orders. But I couldn't do it to you today.'

I thanked him, my mind elsewhere. I learned a little later that the interrogation had indeed taken place with the help of the gendarmes. And that it had essentially consisted of a litany of complaints about me, iterated with great enjoyment by Alfred Sirven.

Closing Salvoes

Renaud Van Ruymbeke and I talked things over one-to-one. I had thought about it for a long time. After six years of carrying out an inquiry in a hostile environment, I had learned to get my priorities straight. The interests of the investigation had to be my sole guideline. Alfred Sirven's lawyers had tried to create a division between us. Renaud had sincerely thought that he would obtain detailed information for the case by summoning Sirven. He had tried and failed. Let he who has never made a mistake cast the first stone.

Renaud offered to withdraw from the case. I refused. There were six months remaining for us to tie up the investigation. The pieces of banking evidence from Switzerland, Jersey and Liechtenstein would soon be sent to us by the local authorities after the appeals had been exhausted. Incorporating them into the dossier would be an exhausting task which I could not undertake alone. Laurence Vichnievsky had asked for a transfer, and Renaud knew every volume of the investigation. He had gone through them one by one with a fine-toothed comb for a year. He had the energy that I had had at the beginning. I would not get there alone, and I needed that fire.

Our differences were not personal. The problem was due to something else entirely.

When Renaud had arrived on the case, the circuits of corruption were out in the open, the principal protagonists defined and their defence had been exposed. All the doors had already been opened. For my part, I was coming from five years in the firing line, in a climate of threats and intimidation which it was impossible to share, both from a sense of propriety and because we were caught up with the work that had yet to be done. Renaud did not notice the electric waves that propagated themselves around me, the permanent interference that flowed from this particular set of circumstances. He lived without a police escort. He took the metro. For him, the case was no longer living matter, but an immense pile of paper. We spoke two languages, which were superposed without mixing. Like oil and water.

Based on the evidence, those indicted had believed for a long time that they would avoid trial. Without a doubt, they were convinced that the obstacles strewn across my path would be insurmountable. Henceforth, it would be every man for himself as they attempted to obtain from the outside a victory which they had not been able to achieve from the inside. They had to discredit me at any price and if possible get me out of the way. The principal actors in the case therefore launched a charm offensive on Renaud, who did not remain impervious to it. It is difficult to be immune to flattery.

The goal was clear: to eliminate me from the game. The risks of destabilisation were increased by the imminence of the closure date; our team could not break up on the closing straight of this marathon. Renaud agreed. We decided to carry out the greater part of the last interrogations together.

Media hold-up

As the preliminary judgement on the Dumas trial approached, friendly magistrates warned me that the Palais de Justice was abuzz with rumours of a general discharge. In my capacity as investigating magistrate, this decision did not concern me. The inquiry and the judgement are two distinct parts of the procedure. That is the rule of the institutions. But I suspected that the decision would have an impact on the climate in which we could close the principal investigation.

A friend who had that week watched *Envoyé spécial* on France 2, told me that she had seen an accusatory dismantling of the investigation, with Loïk Le Floch-Prigent as a character witness. 'I heard your requiem,' she added in a disheartened tone, before hanging up. I, personally, had stopped watching the television or listening to the radio, and made do with the court press digest. For me, the lies no longer stung.

On 30th May 2001, the judgement went against all the predictions disseminated day after day by the 'generally well-informed sources'. It upset the media strategy of those who wanted a favourable decision in the first part of the Elf affair in order to minimise the importance of the investigation still in progress, which represented 90% of the alleged offences.

There was an impassioned reaction from the lawyers. The same evening, a petition circulated demanding my removal from the investigation. It was signed by most of the lawyers for those indicted in the Dumas-Deviers-Joncour case. It concerned, as always, Maître Turcon, but this time in the context of our inquiry into the activities of Alfred Sirven. For months we had explored every opening which presented itself, from the most anecdotal to the most serious. One day during this extremely thorough search, we learned of the existence of a 'blanc' from Special Branch, a confidential document containing unverified information (and thus to be treated with caution) from unidentified sources relating to the former tax counsel to Alfred Sirven.

This rumour was worth no more than the hundreds of others which made their way to us, but we could not discard it without checking it out. This was part of our job as investigating magistrates. There is no sanctuary in the law: being a lawyer does not confer immunity in criminal matters. I ordered that the information be verified. This was taken as a provocation, given the conflict involving myself and Maître Turcon in April 1999, and which was condemned by the Bar.

Thus far, there was nothing illegal about the lawyers' petition, however, it discredited our methods. First of all, it involved the old controversy about the distinction between *tax counsel* (which was then the status of Maître Turcon) and Alfred Sirven's *lawyer* – which he became after our verification was carried out. But most importantly, the petition stated that I had had the lawyer's phone tapped. Had this been the case, it would have been illegal, since I would have had to inform the president of the Bar in advance. This I had not done, simply because I had not requested that Maître Turcon's phone be tapped.

No one called me to verify this information. The following morning, I received a fax from the president of the tribunal. He sent me a copy of a letter from the president of the Bar and demanded an explanation, as if he imagined for one second that the allegations could be true.

Disheartened by the unfairness of it, I decided not to reply immediately. I was giving a lecture in Stockholm the following morning, and had planned to take three days off over Whitsun. I told myself that the president could wait until the following Tuesday. However, I should have remembered the excitement that had followed the complaint from the Bar... Same cause, same effect. The complicity between certain lawyers and accredited journalists intensified their indignant protestations to a worrying degree. The affair took off like a fire in dry grass.

The Parisian circles in which the world is reinvented are very select. They mould reality as they see fit. They organise dinner parties and say what the others want to hear. These people represent the sediment of French history: the cream of the administrative, political, industrial, financial, media and intellectual elite have coopted three boroughs of the capital. A few thousand powerful men and women mingle and interact on a daily basis forming a fast-moving network that accelerates rumours.

I was alarmed on my return from Sweden. The media's indignation was swelling dangerously. My 'unbearable' methods were being disparaged. Le Figaro devoted its front page to the events.[1] Le Monde produced a scandalised editorial. The president of the Bar wrote an insulting article about me. The director of the Nouvel Observateur wrote of his fear: 'Certain media-friendly judges give you a chill up the spine.'

I noted that my supposed criminal behaviour had obscured their judgement. The defendants were the accused, but it was the judge who was guilty! This sort of holding to ransom by the media is a textbook case in communication for lawyers, and a lovely sleight of hand. Although I reproached myself for my peremptory statements which had undermined my position at the time of the storm in April 1999, these unfounded accusations were, nonetheless, very unfair. The Paris Attorney-General published a communiqué which clearly and without reserve explained that telephone tapping of Maître Turcon had never taken place. No paper printed it.

Nobody was interested in the truth.[2]

---

1   The paper talked hypothetically about my recusal: 'The shockwave which has been building for two days could be devastating. [...] From now on it's the Eva Joly scandal!' (Le Figaro, 1st June 2001).

2   The president of the Bar was to refuse to publish a 'right to reply' to his article, in contravention of the right of the press. His intransigence forced me to take legal action, by which it was agreed that I was in the right in April 2003. The president of the Bar appealed against the judgement.

Witch hunt

The investigation was almost complete. My being eliminated from the picture would not change a single one of the suspicious money transfers. The goal of this latest plot, from start to finish, was something else. Everything was being made to look as if the sentence passed on the president of the Constitutional Council – eighteen months in prison, with six months before parole[3] – could not be stomached by the French political and legal systems unless it was simultaneously accompanied by the fall of the investigating magistrate who revealed the scandal. The balance of power comes at such a price.

I replied to the presiding judge of the court. My letter increased the fury of the lawyers. I wrote a column for *Le Monde*. Before sending it, I consulted my friends, who advised me not to intervene publicly.

'It's a witch hunt. The slightest word from you will redouble the attacks. Everything depends on the Justice Minister. Only she can defuse the situation.'

The lid shut back down on me. The president of the magistrates' trade union was pessimistic as to the outcome of the crisis: 'According to our information, the letter to remove you from the case is ready. It just needs the signature of the chief presiding judge of the court of appeal.'

I felt as if I had been checkmated without seeing it coming. It was a nightmare. In the afternoon, one of the defence lawyers on the case knocked on my chambers' door. He was uneasy. 'This is terrible. I didn't anticipate that this would reach such a level.'

'You knew that the tapping never happened.'

'I'm sorry. I had no choice.'

'Did you sign the petition?'

'Yes.'

I stood up, overcome by emotion.

'Get out!'

The following morning I was surprised to hear the lawyer speaking on the radio. He backed down publicly on his signature and distanced himself from his colleagues. A few days later he wrote me a unexpected letter, considering that the end was nigh. When tension reached a peak I

---

3   On appeal, on 29th January 2003, Roland Dumas would be definitively released.

always received many heart-warming letters. However, this missive came from a man who had no reason to treat me with care.

> *Madam Judge, and dear Madam,*
>
> *I have hesitated for a long time before writing these few words, probably because I thought that reason would quickly triumph over excess and tumult. I realise now that the opposite may well happen and that we are now witnessing an orchestration of the media, designed, on the pretext and in the name of the guiding principles of our democracy, to destabilise and sideline you.*
>
> *Before going further, I should like to emphasise my disagreement with the searches carried out by the police in connection with one of my colleagues. But for me, that is not the crux of the matter. There are normal procedures for contesting your decisions and acts, which are within the law.*
>
> *That is not the way that has been chosen, and I regret it.*
>
> *Taking into account my own responsibilities, I should herewith like to convey to you my indignation about what is now emerging. For six years you have investigated this exceptional case with force and determination, but contrary to what certain people would have believed, without ever, even in the most difficult moments, departing from the reserve which is appropriate to your function.*
>
> *Given the fact of our respective positions in this case, we have found ourselves, and we shall find ourselves again, no doubt, in opposition on various points. That is to be expected, given our respective roles and functions. But on the basics, that is to say, in respect of the rights of the defence, I hereby bear witness to your rectitude and your understanding. At no time during the process have I been refused permission to consult the file, or to have a copy of the most recent pieces of evidence, even those which had yet to be catalogued. At no point during the process has the door to your chambers been shut, nor have I been refused the opportunity to discuss the affair and its progress.*
>
> *But the point which I should like most to emphasise is that of the transparency of your action. You always said what you were going to do and did what you said you would do. The unpleasant proceedings which are currently being undertaken against you and the personal attacks revolt me. They are unjust and insufferable.*

Our respective positions as judge and lawyer require distance and reserve, both necessary and obligatory. However, this distance and reserve should not be synonymous with indifference.

In a personal capacity, in my position as lawyer at the Court of Appeal in Paris, I would ask you to accept this expression of my most profound respect for your past, present and future actions.

When we next met I thanked him for his letter. Courageous men exist, and he was one of them. He told me that after his appearance on the radio, he had had to put up with 'a number of violent and threatening phone calls', which he would never have imagined possible. He said no more of it. But once again, I was made aware that outside my case and the visible movements which showed on the surface here and there, subterranean currents were at work with their favourite weapons: intimidation and harassment.

This first dissent from the ranks among the lawyers was the sign that the manoeuvre, however well led, was not assured of victory. The days passed, then weeks, without a reaction from the chancery. I later learned that several high-ranking magistrates had stayed the arm of the Justice Minister.

Although my colleagues had been tarnished by the rumours, the key men in the judiciary responsible for sentencing knew that this financial investigation – unparalleled both with regard to the size of the presumed embezzlements and the unreal atmosphere which had surrounded our inquiry – could not be derailed.

I understood that nothing would happen over the summer.

Safe and Sound

In the autumn of 2001, Laurence Vichnievsky left us to take up the post of presiding judge in Chartres. Her departure was for me the real end of the investigation. I had no time to dwell on my feelings, such was the load of our work programme. Renaud Van Ruymbeke and I surpassed our previous statistics.[1] We led up to three interrogations a day, often together. We worked well together. I prefer concrete and direct volleys of questions. Renaud tends to summarise more and can encapsulate an issue in a few sentences.

Physically, the fact that there were two of us, as had long been the case with Laurence, allowed us to re-establish the equilibrium more easily. When I was investigating the Bernard Tapie affair, I had to battle against the mental influence that the former Minister for Urban Affairs, who is now an actor, had over others. By his way of moving, of making his presence felt, and with his expressive features and quick mind, he absorbed the power in a room. The experience taught us to compensate for such phenomena by tirelessly coming back to the facts and to our task, without allowing ourselves to be intimidated or bewitched too much by unusual personalities.

Hostility emanated from the powerful men who filed through our chambers that summer in the company of their lawyers. They made it clear that their place was not here, but at the board of director's table. In extreme situations – and when a man risks ten years in prison, he is in a state of absolute awareness – human beings give off unusual vibes. You must draw on your inner strength, focus solely on the facts and ignore the verbal violence directed at you.

---

1 These accounting summaries list the judicial activities carried out by each chambers and allow our system to supervise our rate of work.

The attempts at destabilisation continued. A lawyer told me that he had been approached to draw up a partnership between two parties in exchange for several tens of millions of francs. That no longer surprised me. After seven years of investigation, nothing was beyond the realm of the imagination. I knew that the incredible was possible.

The interrogations were extremely tense, with endless procedural problems. I witnessed some astonishing scenes. During a confrontation between Alfred Sirven and André Tarallo, we suspended the hearing for a few minutes to look for a piece of evidence in the archives.

I then heard this extraordinary dialogue, conducted in a conversational tone, between Alfred Sirven and his lawyer:

Maître Turcon: 'Another bastard of a pro-judge journalist has written an article against us in *Le Point*.'

Alfred Sirven: 'But how is it that there are still pro-judge journalists about? I thought the problem had been sorted…'

Maître Turcon: 'Don't worry. He's been dealt with. His career is over.'

The clerk, those indicted and the lawyers looked at each other in astonishment. Vulgar speech is rare in chambers. But more than that, it was their arrogance which shocked me, their way of behaving within sight and hearing of everyone, as though the press were a business of mutual networks and intimidation.

I could not call the President of the Bar to record the incident, because things were contentious between us since the editorial in which he painted me as 'a danger to democracy'. Getting the president of the court to intervene seemed to be risky after the two hostile letters I had received from him. Therefore, I let the incident pass.

A page turns

At that point I began to think about my future. After the closure of the Elf case, it seemed to me that it would be difficult to continue to exercise the same functions. I owed my professional survival to the free will of the Justice Minister. My relationship with certain big names of the Bar had reached a crisis point. It was not a healthy situation.

More importantly, I knew that the Elf case had been able to prosper and reach this size because of a little miracle due to the timing, the circumstances, a lucky sequence of events and some fortunate meetings.

But the investigation was underneath a volcano. An institution cannot function in these restrictive circumstances.

The Elf case was the end of an era, but it also marked the end of the line. All the signs indicated that the country would not go beyond this point. It was as if French democracy had reached the limit of the revelations that it could bear. However, Elf had not accounted for, from 1990-1993, all the alleged offences of all those in power in the country. Our inquiry was like a drill uncovering deeply buried layers. Compared with other scandals of the time, it confirmed the extent of a culture of corruption where breaking the law is no longer an issue.

The philosopher René Girard has stressed the point to which our societies are mimetic. Each embezzlement, by imitation, results in another which itself contaminates its neighbour. This is the sequence which has to be broken. The reality exposed by the investigation was probably too cruel for the country to bear. Neither the law nor French society was ready to hear the truth.

The Elf investigation had navigated through muddy waters but the probability of landing safe and sound in port was almost nil. How many magistrates would be ready, tomorrow, to put themselves into the tunnel that we went through for seven years, and to pay the price that we paid? I strongly doubt that they would drink the poison offered to them. If guilty plea reforms currently under discussion in parliament had been applicable in 1994 there would perhaps have been no Elf affair, but a simple transaction between the prosecutor and the protagonists of the Bidermann case: a fine and several months in prison with a reprieve for good behaviour. The majority of the alleged offences that we had uncovered would have remained buried in the accounts of Elf.

Abroad, there was a general ebbing of enthusiasm. The action by the Geneva prosecutor, Bernard Bertossa, came to an end in Switzerland upon the election of his successor, who was more inclined to concentrate his efforts on the fight against pickpocketing. On the other side of the Alps, the Italian magistrates were violently criticized by the political elite. In Rome, one of the most indicted company directors in Italy had become head of state.[2] In

---

2   Apart from proceedings pending at the time of writing, Silvio Berlusconi has already been convicted for perjury in connection with the P2 lodge (an offence covered by the amnesty of 1989), sentenced on first hearing to 33 months in prison for bribery (offence lapsed on appeal), sentenced to 28 months in prison for illegal financing of a political party (offence lapsed on appeal and cassation), and to 16 months in prison for false accounting (offence lapsed on appeal), (cf. *Le Monde*, 22nd March 2002).

France, numerous politicians were triumphantly re-elected after serving their sentences. One of them, sentenced for corruption, defended, in the Senate, repressive amendments to reinforce the presumption of innocence.

A page was turning in Europe, after ten years of turmoil.

Several humanitarian organisations offered me positions on their board of directors. I myself was tempted to move on to something new. But I didn't feel as if I had run my course. My interest in the accounts of the oil company had transformed me intellectually. I had seen impunity as the rule and the law as the exception. I had measured the limits of the law. Unfortunately, it was not because we would no longer be pursuing financial offences that they would no longer be a menace to the social contract – on the contrary. My conscience would not leave me in peace. I wanted to be useful, even if I did not yet know where or how.

Secret meetings

It only took one meeting. On 15th October 2001, the Norwegian publisher William Nygaard gave a party to mark the launch of my book in Oslo. We were in the patrician villa which belonged to his family, at the banks of a fjord, overlooking a large garden, which the autumn had splashed with gold. The place was a step back into history, with its library, its glittering silverware, its armchairs covered in old velvet… I was in a bubble, far from the hostile world where so many forces wanted to see us fail.

It was the eve of the constitution of a new government. My publisher introduced me to Odd Einar Dørum, who was to become the new Minister of Justice the following day. He explained to me that he had followed my activities for a long time. The Norwegian leadership had, for several years, felt an increasing need for a stricter international rule to deal with corruption. They had heard of several lectures I had given in Paris to Scandinavian diplomats.

'Your ideas interest me, Mrs Joly. I think we could do something together. We must meet again.'

I didn't pay much attention to this potential opportunity. Thirty years of life in Paris had made me philosophical about this sort of casual comment, which leaders in Paris often made to their listeners, as if throwing seeds to the birds. I was to learn later that the idea had been making its way round the circles of the Norwegian administration and that Odd Einar Dørum had already talked it over with the future Minister for Foreign Affairs, Jan Petersen.

At the beginning of November, I was contacted by the new Secretary of State for Justice. We had a preliminary meeting to set out the basis for a future collaboration. I went to Norway four times to refine our project. I had requested total confidentiality. I wanted first of all to finish the Elf investigation and tie up another pending case - IBSA bank – in order to leave everything tidy in France. We met in secret at my publisher's house as we were still at the negotiation stage.

Odd Einar Dørum is one of those politicians no longer common in Europe, one who is more concerned with the fate of the world than with his career. He wasn't in it for himself. 'Norway is an important player in the area of development aid. We are among the biggest contributors in the world. We have a real role amongst the international institutions. Corruption has become a constantly pressing matter. Do you think we can do something?'

We swapped ideas for hours on end. I was not going to reinvent the wheel. Several hundred experts had traced out the broad picture; whole bookshelves could be filled by reports written on the matter. But I could contribute by applying key measures at strategic points drawn from my own experience. We sketched the outlines of what would become my mission and our project. I saw light at the end of the tunnel. For the first time in months, I felt that I was talking the same language as a politician.

At the beginning of December 2001, I warned Renaud Van Ruymbeke of my decision. He was the first person I told. From then on, he knew that once the case was closed and the charges made by the public prosecutor's department, he would be the one drawing up the order of transfer. I had every confidence in him. When I met Laurence Vichnievsky again, who had already returned to the practical concerns of a provincial court, she encouraged me in my decision, with a bit of envy in her voice: 'Not everyone is lucky enough to have dual nationality…'

The speck and the plank

In the middle of December, cases of documents reached us from Switzerland. We unfolded the huge summary diagrams drawn up by Paul Perraudin, which were models of precision and attention to detail. We worked without stopping, without raising our heads. It was the final big push.

At the end of January 2002, we tied up the investigation. An extraordinary tale of eight years was at an end. I put a full stop on the dozens of searches and letters rogatory, the thousands of hearings and statements, the piles of expert evidence... This mountain of paper had physically retained a part of me.

The comments in the press were muted, as was to be expected, given how hard it is to understand such a complex affair, and especially one so controversial and drawn-out. In financial matters, the perfect investigation does not exist. Several leads were lost in the shifting sands of the tax havens. A section on the suspect movements of funds could not be pieced together given the degree of banking confidentiality and collusion surrounding secret accounts.

Our investigations had also had to take account of diplomatic immunity. The law protects heads of state from any petition. The personal accounts of monarchs, presidents elected for life or dictators supported by electoral manipulation are protected from the curiosity of judges. Money can come in and go out of their coffers with the assurance that no one will come and stick their nose into possible trafficking. All the same, the truth about the allocation of several hundreds of millions of francs given in cash to Alfred Sirven remained a mystery, because he did not wish to explain what he had used it for. We could not be sure, either, that the principal defendants were the sole beneficiaries of the embezzled funds. But they had chosen to take responsibility for the totality of the suspect movements of cash and we could go no further without their cooperation.

Reading the disillusioned comments, I found it paradoxical that we were accused of having looked for the speck in the eye of some whilst neglecting the plank in that of their neighbour. The speck in question was worth several tens of millions of francs a head, for a total of several billion. The plank was always completely out of reach...

To investigate is to follow a reasonable path. Even achieving this much had not been easy – at several points we had nearly lost everything.[3] After

---

3   I should like to note the decisive contribution made by the following magistrates of the public prosecutor's department: François Franqui, Anne-José Fulgéras, Jean-Pierre Champrenault and Jean-Claude Marin. And, on the Bench, the unfailing support of the chief vice-president of the court, Claude Noquet. Without them, the Elf affair would never have finished.

the closing of the inquiry, so dense was the case – successive layers and piece upon piece of evidence - that four people were engaged full time to draw up the charges. The first instance and appeal hearings would spread out over several months. I was happy with that speck.

Some commentators expressed regret that we had not launched full-scale investigations into ten years of French secret policy, or exposed the threads of Françafrique, those incestuous links between France and her former colonies, or gone into the links between the arms trade and 'parallel diplomacy'. All that from our office? It was unimaginable.

But I, too, still had the feeling that one should not stop at the threshold of the law. One should go further and get into the political sphere, where the order of things can be changed. The offer from the Norwegian government could not have been more opportune.

One evening I met a lawyer with whom I had a relationship of mutual respect. We went for a drink in a café. He told me the latest news from the Palais de Justice, the *combinazione*, the arrogance of the networks, the derisory agreements and the big negotiations that were part of his daily life. I stared at him. He began to laugh.

'But that's France! You wanted to change France, but that's impossible…'

His giggles were infectious. But he was wrong, all the same. I had never had the illusion that I could have changed France; neither from my cupboard of an office that lacked both fax and computer, nor, later, in the luxurious offices of the financial investigation unit, that empty shell which was so impressive from the outside but had the same restricted means for carrying out inquiries. I had battled to get to the end of my investigation despite the decadent state of the world that I had uncovered. I had not wanted cynicism and the law of the powerful few to win the day. That was all. Despite my mistakes, I felt as if I had done my duty. And even if I had not changed France, my adopted country had changed me. It had taught me a great deal, sometimes reluctantly: I was going back to Norway with the eyes of a Frenchwoman.

At the beginning of June 2002, I left my office. I bade farewell to my police escort, to my assistant Serge, and to my friends in the Palais de Justice. Strangely, although I was sad at leaving the pleasures of the banks of the Seine and the little streets of St-Germain-des-Prés, a weight fell from my shoulders when the plane took off. Shortly after landing at Oslo airport, I got on a bicycle. Henceforth without police protection, free to do what I wished, my first instinctive action was to pedal to the sea.

At that point, I couldn't yet manage to feel happy, as I was still profoundly upset; there were emotions buried in my heart that I had not been able to set free. I breathed the sea air down to the bottom of my lungs, like one who had almost been suffocated. My mind was numb. I repeated to myself, 'It's over, it's over…' I realised that the threats to my integrity over eight years had profoundly marked me.

Over the next weeks, I got to know certain everyday situations again, one after the other: coming back alone to my home, travelling at night, stopping on a snow-covered road to open a barrier… But I still feel the after-effects of that lengthy period spent in the vicinity of danger. I take certain precautions which seem incongruous out of context. Sometimes, in a sudden rush, I may feel the poison of fear creeping in my veins, from the brain to the heart. I see myself as a fugitive in full daylight, with a target painted on my back. Then I have to focus on the present and not let myself be overwhelmed with painful memories.

Another World

Leaving Paris, where the activities of ten million busy men and women gave off an invisible electricity, to go back to provincial Oslo, by the sea, was soothing. Norway, with its land area at different latitudes, its prosperity and its obsession with nature is somehow removed from major world changes and financial globalisation.

Situated on the edge of a majestic fjord, its capital cultivates the mastery of emotions.

I had a completely clean slate in my new job, where I was beginning a three-year term as advisor to the Ministers for Justice and Foreign Affairs. I was not heading up an administration and I was succeeding no one. I had to choose my team.[1] The smallest of my decisions was like a footprint on fresh snow.

On the political timescale, three years is an incredibly short period of time. My friends in the Norwegian administration warned me: if I made ill-judged choices at the beginning, the structures were so legendarily unwieldy that I would spend months trying to recover from a weak position. We should then arrive at the end of my mission without the smallest tangible result.

There was a certain logic to the idea that I install my team in the Ministry of Foreign Affairs, where the high-level diplomats work, often involved in numerous delicate negotiations, like the Israeli-Palestinian

---

1 In particular, I recruited Anne-Mette Dyrnes, first assistant public prosecutor in the national section for the struggle against criminal financial activity, in charge of the Norwegian delegation to the Financial Action Task Force on money laundering (FATF); Atle Roaldsøy, first assistant public prosecutor, responsible for the Norwegian delegation to Greco (Council of Europe); and Unn Torgersen, responsible for documentation and organisation.

conflict, and regularly in the thick of the creation of great international conventions. The history goes back a long way. Norway had signed bilateral agreements for the prevention of piracy several decades before the first international convention of Utrecht for maritime commerce in 1740. Our national hero, Nansen, was a diplomat from the times of the First World War who spent his life raising the profile of refugees, committed himself to working against the famine in the newly-created USSR and denounced the Armenian genocide.[2]

The Nobel Peace Prize is awarded in Oslo. For better or for worse, Norwegians are convinced they have a role to play in bringing a better quality of life to the world. Their almost mythical alliance with nature makes them viscerally hostile to disorder of any sort: war, poverty, pollution or corruption. *De facto*, the quality of its diplomacy gives Norway a weight in international affairs out of all proportion with its real power.

In giving me this mission, the government was demonstrating its desire to have an influence on international choices, and so I could have joined the ranks of the Foreign Affairs. But in order for our voice to be heard beyond our boundaries, we had to be anchored in the reality of the country. How powerful can words be if they are not immediately relevant to oneself? I chose, therefore, to join the Ministry of Justice.

Changing skin

The building was one of those monuments to the triumphant Labour philosophy of the 1950s, which evoke a feeling of power and not grace. The austerity of the place was reinforced by the particular security of our offices, which had been built in such a way as to prevent phone-tapping or clandestine photography. I was entitled to defence secrecy: I had to be able to receive visitors in total security. By one of those twists of fate which add to the flavour of life, I was from now on fully protected in Oslo, where I could work with complete transparency on open cases. In contrast, while I was at risk when investigating the embezzlement of several billion francs, my Parisian offices were never protected.

---

2   The Armenian Genocide was carried out by the 'Young Turk' government of the Ottoman Empire in 1915-1916 (with subsidiaries to 1922-23). One and a half million Armenians were killed, out of a total of two and a half million in the Ottoman Empire.

One morning I found myself in an empty room, with three pencils, an immaculate blotter and a brand new computer. I had to start from the beginning and recruit a team from among the dozens of high-level candidates, draw up proposals, outline a plan of attack. Beginning a new life at fifty-eight years of age is a unique opportunity. I have done a lot of jobs in my life: a young au pair, secretary, legal advisor in a psychiatric hospital, assistant public prosecutor, recorder to the Ministry of Finance, investigating magistrate, and now here I was, a government advisor. Passing from one world to another is endlessly enriching: it's like adding a splash of colour to a Harlequin's coat.

I had spent the last seven years in a trance; each day on arriving at the office I would have to sort out the pile of 'urgent' files, look left and right for enemies skulking in the shadows, my mind permanently occupied by a convoluted case. The absence of such concerns now allowed me to work without the added pressure of struggling for survival.

I had to carry out a Copernican revolution. I was no longer a judge, buried under detail, but a political advisor. I had to embrace a wider world. Having had several jobs and having lived in two different cultures has led me to approach change in a particular way. I begin on the assumption that I know nothing and that I must learn everything from those around me. For weeks, I soaked up information.

In spring 2002, some weeks before leaving France, I met informally in Paris with men and women who held key positions in the economic sector, some from the management team of a large bank, others in finance, on the board of directors of national firms or in tax management. I spent hours with well-known experts in money laundering.

In a straightforward manner I asked them, in confidence, for an assessment of corruption in France and their views on how it should be tackled. The question seemed to be of the highest importance for all of them. But, to hear them talk, the corruptor was always someone else: he or she who did the job from over there. For corruption is a secret of the initiated which is played with few players. Rare are those who have the opportunity of entering into the heart of things, behind the facades, and who return from it. Our elite are intellectually powerless when faced with this question. Here and there I picked up information that would be useful to me.

In Norway, I followed the same approach. I was eager for everything. I had to learn what things remained unsaid in Norway, since every society is defined by its implicit rules. What I had loved about France, the courtesy, the banter, the elegance, the culture, a certain refinement, all of that no longer held sway. I rediscovered the importance given to equality, serious-mindedness pushed to the extreme, a taste for self-improvement, a primitive need for nature, the courage to live in an environment that is hostile eight months of the year.

I also had to mentally adjust to my new life. Returning to one's native land after thirty-five years of life abroad is a major step. I was not exactly the same person, but I was not exactly someone else either. In the early days, the past and the present constantly overlapped before my eyes, as if two pieces of tracing paper had been placed one on top of the other and then moved slightly out of line. I rediscovered childhood friends, and experiences buried deep in my subconscious. The language had evolved: I spoke a Norwegian that was a little out of place. I translated literally from the French much to the amusement of those I spoke to.

First click

I was surrounded by joyful goodwill as I was adapting to my new life. I needed some weeks to get used to such kindness. The press had warmly greeted my nomination. For them, I was a 'Huntress of Corruption', based on the title my publisher chose for my book. There were friendly smiles everywhere. The magistrates and the police who specialised in combating financial fraud spoke to me of their own accord. They asked me for advice and used me as a hotline for sensitive inquiries, relying on my interest in and my experience of clandestine issues.

In my native land, my name, which had attracted so much hostility in France, was synonymous with commitment. This honour was all the greater because the Norwegians had not had to call themselves into question and were still living under the illusion that financial wrongdoing stopped at their borders. Like other magistrates before me, such as Baltasar Garzón in Spain, Antonio Di Pietro in Italy, or Bernard Bertossa in Switzerland, I discovered that anti-corruption judges are as much praised abroad as they are denigrated and attacked in their own countries. When magistrates investigate those in power, they upset the order of things. Thanks to my dual nationality, in Oslo I escaped the ritual maledictions that I had known in Paris.

After some weeks, I had a meeting in Washington in September 2002 with the committee of the International Monetary Fund (IMF) responsible for combating corruption. I was not at my best on that particular morning. I would go as far as to say that I was quite average, thanks to a combination of bronchitis and jet lag. To my great surprise, I was to receive many moving emails in which the authors wrote that my contribution had 'given them energy for ten years' or that they would 'never forget that meeting'. Nonetheless, my listeners, comprising big thinkers and international experts, had not been knocked over by my knowledge; rather, it had been the hope engendered by the new Norwegian policy.

For a year, I have often noticed a similar phenomenon, even if, fortunately, I manage to be more switched on than I was in the offices of the IMF. In Mexico, I was received by Parliament and the judicial authorities. In the corridors of the UN, African diplomats rushed to congratulate and encourage me. In Bulgaria, the rooms where I spoke were completely full. In India, with Bernard Bertossa, the former prosecutor in Geneva, we trained magistrates who had come from all over the subcontinent, and who in turn were confronting the obstacles that we had faced ten years earlier in our inquiries into corruption. My office received daily requests for interviews or conferences from all over the world.

On a personal level this would have been perfect retribution for the hostility visited upon me at the Palais de Justice in Paris. It would be enough for me to go with the flow and spend three years passing from auditorium to auditorium. It would not have been a blow to my ego. I would even have felt like I was doing something. But it would have been a complete betrayal of the Norwegian government and those citizens seeking justice across the world.

So, on the contrary, my work consisted of fulfilling the hope that citizens placed in us. This was nothing to be afraid of. Action is propelled by will, like in judo. We had to be like 'particle accelerators' and champion four or five big reforms which could change what was taken for granted, and lessen the impunity of the powerful.

In chemistry, a heterogeneous element is all that is required to produce a catalytic reaction. In chemical terms, I am this parasite, an outsider in the usual power structure. I had to immerse myself in these ideas and disregard personal reward. If I relied on the support of my listeners to satisfy my interests, I would be destroyed. In order to be in with a chance of winning the game, there had to be nothing to gain, neither for me nor for Norway.

Large-scale corruption

On entering diplomatic circles, I retained the mindset of an investigating magistrate to the closest degree, like the character in Bunyan's *Pilgrim's Progress* who preferred to scrape the dirt from the ground rather than raise his eyes skyward. I didn't forget my roots.

I discovered the world of international negotiations. The UN building in Vienna, on the edge of the city, was an immense and impressive building. Thousands of civil servants from all over the world walked the corridors. There was endless chatter in every language. I met legal experts who knew the subtleties of the law, and were able to find solutions suited to every legal system.

Marathon meetings between experts are an astonishing spectacle. Every word is a battle. Lengthy negotiations might only result in the moving of few commas or one or two adjectives. Lacking the mandate to make decisions of substance, I tried to bring the force of my conviction and my experience to meetings in the corridors, the ambassadorial dinners and the hotel breakfasts, where alliances are made and unmade. With my colleagues in the delegation, we formed an energetic team..

It was evident that the battle against corruption was colossal, given the natural inclination of these institutions towards consensus. I tried to talk as straightforwardly as possible, which came as a surprise to some. Diplomats are experts at saying things without entirely spelling them out. When they needed to give an example, they tended to talk about Uurdistan, an imaginary country like something from the adventures of Tintin. At least in this case there was no chance of offending any ambassador. I don't refer to Uurdistan. I say things like they are.

125

When a delegation wished to speak, the custom was to raise the little flag of their country on the table in front of them. One day, at the Organisation for Economic Co-operation and Development (OECD), I had begun speaking in my usual direct way to request the removal of judges' immunity from prosecution. I had hardly begun my speech when dozens of little flags were raised. But I continued speaking about my trip to the East and the gravity of the problem of corrupt judges, who, since the days of communism, were all too often in the habit of selling their decisions for a few unearned advantages. The example helped. At the end of my contribution, all the flags were lowered.

It was often the case that after a few seconds of wavering people would speak freely, and warm to the topic. The discussions would frequently move beyond official limits, abandoning frosty professionalism and its associated Newspeak.

The world of Mr Happy

I quickly realised that the international conventions had one fault. They were drawn up by honest people, conscientious civil servants who moved from aeroplane to meeting room and back again. Most of them were devoted to the common good. But they lived in a bubble in their institutions. Corruption and money laundering was another world. They were fighting with a non-existent enemy. And all the time it was there, beside them, sometimes at the very heart of their government.

One day I paid a visit to the Norwegian police academy. We watched a practice operation. In a mocked-up stage set, the students learned how to search a drug dealer's flat: they had to make a surprise entrance and rush towards the toilet door to stop the trafficker flushing away his stock of cocaine. But no test had been envisaged to catch the banker laundering money in his office. Customs inspectors have dogs to detect cocaine, but they are of no use where numbered bank accounts are concerned. Such an exercise would require an entirely different stage set. They would have had to get rid of the shabby wallpaper and the sachets of powder behind the enamel toilet bowl and instead install an office of steel and exotic wood, with a three-inch thick angora carpet and computers connected to the international clearing houses. As the Spanish judge Baltasar Garzón joked, nobody bothers holding up a bank any more: they just buy it. When crime is at the top, everything gets complicated.

The old tale of the man who loses his keys one night, and then only looks for them under the streetlight, where the pavement is lit, applies perfectly to the law. Although it's a truism to say so, we only find where we seek. However, large-scale corruption is invisible, embedded in the heart of power where one would least expect to find it. The chief executive of Enron was one of the great figures of American capitalism, still cited as an example in the financial press only a few weeks before being photographed in handcuffs. Financial crime does not show itself: you have to look for it, to scratch away at the surface.

The mind cries out in protest when asked to accept that widespread corruption exists. The philosopher Alain Finkielkraut, a big opponent of financial investigations and a perfect spokesperson for the French elite, has suggested a simple alternative: 'Either you focus on scandals or you focus on 'normal business'.'[1] Corruption, then, is not a political matter but a minor issue which pollutes the public debate.

This view is comfortable but absurd. Large-scale corruption is at the heart of 'normal business' and not on its periphery. In the Elf case, there was not a right and a wrong way of conducting business, but a complete overlapping of corporate strategy and financial wrongdoing. All key decisions, whether related to negotiations for petroleum exploration, the purchase of concessions, insurance policies or property acquisitions gave rise to clandestine monetary transactions. We have to face up to this reality; otherwise it will be too late.

The pessimism of Vaclav Havel, an intellectual who held a powerful position, is a serious wake-up call. Upon leaving his position in the Czech Republic, he stated: 'Mafioso capitalism extends to every level of the state, and I don't know if there is time to halt its progress. Considerable sums have been passed from hand to hand; incredibly sophisticated methods have been developed with the sole goal of embezzling thousands of dollars. It is a major concern.'[2] But it is probably more reassuring to persuade oneself, like the European elite, that normal business is not altered by the system of corruption.

---

1 'Justice et politique: l'impossible cohabitation?', *Panoramiques*, no. 63, 2003, p.98.
2 'Justice et politique: l'impossible cohabitation?', p.98.

Why such denial? When Norway was looking to broaden EU legislation requiring various sensitive professions (lawyers, auditors etc.) to report any money laundering of which they had knowledge, an important lawyer became alarmed at the totalitarian risks involved in this project. His name, literally meaning 'happy' is not made-up and he wrote his article in his village of three thousand inhabitants, at the foot of a bucolic green mountain of the kind that can only be found in the Great North.

I would like to live in 'Happy' and Finkielkraut's world, a democracy where normal business would bring about essential debate, where heads of state would not open foreign bank accounts, where bankers and auditors would all respect the law, but I have the feeling that they themselves do not know which world they live in. It is of course possible to keep our blinkers on and continue to walk around in a dream. That is not my choice. We have to think about corruption; we have to extract the meaning of it, as one squeezes the juice from a bunch of grapes.

Ten years to change my mind

Before the Elf case, I would not have been capable of formulating matters in such a direct manner. Up to the age of fifty, I was one of those who believed in the greatness of the institutions and the nobility of power. I am not ashamed of this long period of naivety; it was backed up by my daily experience of French society. I have been a legal advisor in a psychiatric hospital and a magistrate in a Parisian suburb. For a long time I was immersed in the medical world. It was not a tranquil world; illness, madness and crime have taught me about the infinite fragility of human beings, and about their secret shadowy side. It makes me think of the Giacometti statue, spindly, unbalanced, on the verge of keeling over, which the sculptor named *Man Walking*. You have to have been one of those who go round sweeping up the stragglers to get close to a certain sort of human frailty.

Nevertheless, during those years I lived in a world where words had meaning. I met doctors who cared for everyone, without thinking about money; psychiatrists, policemen, educators and magistrates who did their job simply and with integrity. When I belonged to a Ministry of Finance commission which aimed to save businesses on the brink of bankruptcy, we moved heaven and earth to find solutions. Then I knew true captains of industry and high-flying civil servants, and I didn't feel like I was operating in a puppet theatre.

I belonged to the great mass of average citizens who work for a regular salary, pay their taxes, respect the law apart from the odd minor infraction and don't question anything. So for a long time I thought that the corruption of the powerful was a minor problem. After all, as Oscar Wilde said, 'It is only shallow people who do not judge by appearance'. It took me ten years to change my mind.

My first shock was the interrogation of Pierre Conso, the chief executive of Ciments Français, a prominent firm which was the third biggest player in the world cement market. At the time we were investigating alleged insider trading which had facilitated the setting up of a secret account abroad. Conso was sincerely astonished by my surprise. I can still see his raised eyebrows as he said to me: 'You must be the only judge not to know that capitalism is built on insider trading! Every firm in the French stock exchange index has a secret account...' He spoke with a sort of resigned exasperation, like a university lecturer talking to a novice.

Of course, an offender's first defence, whether he's wearing a leather jacket or a tailored suit, is always the ritual 'everyone does it', which is supposed to exonerate him from his responsibility. I could have knocked his defence over with the back of my hand. Nonetheless, he was being sincere; he was an entrepreneur, not a predator.

The second shock came when I was working on the tables drawn up by our opposite number in Geneva, Paul Perraudin, dealing with the alleged embezzlements in the Elf case. For the first time, the movement of money in Switzerland by a large company (at the time the number one company in France) was mapped out in detail: over three years the alleged embezzlements totalled more than two and a half billion francs, or half the annual profit of the firm. I was no longer looking at a marginal activity, but at an entire system. This almost peaceful, routine predation – it went as far as the maintenance contracts for aeroplanes hired by Elf – had unfolded without setting off either internal warnings or any rumours amongst the competition. As though it was normal.

We are hiding the truth

I wanted to understand the extent of what we had discovered. Nothing had prepared us for this disturbing reality, and our individual experiences of it were patchy. I had therefore decided to take a step back and to remove myself from the judicial case to look for the key to understanding the whole picture. My frustration was as great as my desire to learn. Although the corrupt activities of those in power makes a good topic for cheap pamphlets and the rhetoric of activists with a bold turn of phrase, it is all too rarely grounds for real reflection.

On an intellectual level, the work of Edwin Sutherland on white-collar crime, dating from 1933, is applicable seventy years later, even though the shape of the economic and social landscape has been completely altered by globalisation.[3] In France, a few rare parliamentary commissions of inquiry have added to our knowledge.[4] But financial crime is still seen only as a subject for a few words in the inside pages of the newspapers, although it is a political fact.

International reports add to the confusion. They juggle with abstract concepts or enormous statistics (as frightening as they are nebulous) on the mafia, whilst my experience of legal cases has been more ambivalent. I have not been confronted by a modern day Hydra, some sort of obviously threatening protean creature, but by a respectable and established power which has simply incorporated large-scale corruption as a natural extra dimension to its activities.

An American journalist gave a striking account of the tale of Enron, the electricity brokering company whose collapse has led Wall Street to undertake the most profound questioning of itself since the crash of 1929: 'There were two completely different sides to the story – the public image, polished by its most senior officers, of an innovative powerhouse on the verge of reshaping the world, and the hidden truth of a company plagued by secrets. It was like a gleaming ocean liner which appeared to be powering forward with its passengers dining in luxury, while, below the waterline, its sweaty crew were frantically bailing the incoming water.'[5] These two tales were in fact one and the same.

---

3   In France, there is also the pioneering work of Pierre Lascoumes (*Elites irrégulières*, Gallimard, 2000), Jean de Maillard (*Un monde sans loi*, already cited) and Yves Meny (*La corruption politique*, Fayard, 1992).

4   cf. the remarkable – and solitary - efforts of the *Mission d'information sur les obstacles au contrôle et à la repression de la délinquance financière et du blanchiment des capitaux en Europe*, led by Vincent Peillon and Arnaud Montebourg, or the conscientious work of the *Mission d'information sur le rôle des companies pétrolières dans la politique internationale*, presided over by Marie-Hélène Aubert.

5   *The New York Times*, 10th February 2002.

Our grasp of the phenomenon is distorted by our need to hide it. Large-scale corruption is always presented as an exception, a mistake, and not as the system it has become. Every commentator on the Elf trial included the obligatory paragraph on 'the bygone days of these detestable practices'. We are pretending that the nature of power is not at all altered by the crime which has been committed in its heart, with its blessing.

It is as if that which ought not to be happening – our betrayal by the elite – is banished from our minds by a sort of collective blindness. The word 'scandal' comes from the Greek 'skandalon', meaning 'trap' or 'obstacle'. We live with the scandals as if they were a trap to avoid or an obstacle to climb over. We hide the truth which flows from them. The subject is declared closed before the debate has even taken place.

The end of the scandals

In Italy, the political powers and the law had fought over the closing of the chapter of the *Mani Pulite*.[6] Those in power simply adapted and took control again. Silvio Berlusconi, the richest man in Italy who had become prime minister after a spectacular campaign, overturned laws that had been created to lengthen the duration of financial offences, repatriate illegal capital and removed, *de facto*, certain offences such as false accounting. As Dario Fo, recipient of the Nobel Prize for Literature, has written, 'We are face-to-face with the most insane paradox, something worthy of Alfred Jarry's *Ubu Roi*, a farce of the impossible: we are making laws just for the king, we are choosing ministers in his court and they are defending his interests alone. The conscience of the Cavaliere and his employees is clear, and he holds all the power, and enjoys total impunity.'[7] In France, the government also attempted to block the ramifications of the scandals. According to the detractors of financial law, these interminable investigations had impugned

---

6   Launched in 1992 by magistrates in Milan, in the front line of whom was Antonio Di Pietro, the *Mani Pulite* (Clean Hands) investigation had brought to light the generalised corruption affecting the Italian party political system. Dealing at the beginning with a notable socialist caught red-handed engaging in corrupt activities, the inquiry had unveiled the widespread bribery in the matter of allocation of public markets (with commission payments of 10-20 % of each contract). Arrests and trials blew the Socialist and Christian Democrat parties to pieces.

7   *Le Monde*, 11th January 2002.

the honour of several scapegoats who had been victims of 'Robespierre-style justice'. Suspicion has led to the creation of a financial investigation unit which has accomplished very little even though it had all the resources, equipment and facilities necessary for its inquiry, explains Alain Finkielkraut who, lacking precise knowledge of his subject, makes up for it with vindictiveness.[8]

The turn of events in France and Italy should not distort our judgement. The judicial 'scandals' were only the beginning of a vast power shift.

Before our very eyes, a metamorphosis was under way.

The philosopher Hume advocated extracting oneself from the minute variations of our perception and the here and now to enter, eyes half-closed, into a sort of indifference to everyday things. Inattention to detail enables one to distinguish the reality of the world.[9] When you go up a level, another reality comes into view. And then one can see the true extent of the change.

According to the Milan public prosecutor's department, large-scale corruption among Italian leaders reached, in ten years, 500 billion lira (about 258 million euros).[10] Since 1990, the Italian magistrates have charged 5000 people (including 338 deputies, 873 entrepreneurs and 1373 civil servants) and sent 3200 people before the courts – where over 90% were found guilty.[11] Despite this unprecedented effort, what the Italians call the *Tagentopoli* (the city of bribery) has not disappeared. Still more recently, thirty-one people – civil servants and company directors – have been implicated in a corruption scandal involving Anas, the public body which deals with the road network; a case of flagrant bribery.[12]

In France, in the course of the last decade, more than 900 elected representatives have been indicted (67.6% for financial offences), including 34 out of 128 ministers or secretaries of state – nearly a quarter

---

8   op.cit., p.98. Two points: the resources at our disposition were limited and as for accomplishing very little, the financial investigation unit uncovered the Elf affair which included financial offences of up to hundreds of millions of Euros, and the inquiry into Angolagate, which already involved a hundred million Euros in suspect funds.
9   'Carelessness and inattention alone can afford us any remedy,' in *A Treatise of Human Nature*.
10   Quoted in *Libération*, 7th December 1994.
11   cf. *La Reppublica*, 6th March 1997, and *L'Hebdo*, 28th February, 2002
12   Agence France-Presse,12th February 2003.

of them![13] The President of the Republic faces a number of charges at the end of his term of office.

In Spain, some years ago, scandals brought about the fall of the socialist leadership. In 2002, an investigation focusing on a large secret account - more than 225 million euros of secret funds placed in Jersey and Liechtenstein – implicated the country's top banking institution, BBVA, in activities involving money-laundering and bribery of Latin American leaders. In Argentina, the financial crisis has been revelatory, like when a pond is suddenly emptied of its water and the silt, buried roots and fish from the depths are brought to light. The full extent of the corruption and dubious financial manipulations was revealed. The situation had reached such proportions that the representative in Argentina of the American Drug Enforcement Administration (DEA) commented that 'if all the scandals were brought out into the open, half the country would be implicated.'[14] For her part, the deputy Elisa Carrio, head of the commission of parliamentary inquiry, officially condemned 'the existence of a criminal matrix whose impunity is guaranteed at the summit of the Supreme Court, with agreements between parties or former and current post-holders.'[15]

In Peru, the strong man of the regime, Vladimiro Montesinos, the power behind President Fujimori, was the object of 70 charges from corruption to arms trafficking. During the inquiry, he was found to be in possession of more than 800 video cassettes showing illicit payments that he was keeping as a hold over those with whom he had had dealings. The legal authorities reckoned that he was at the root of 'a vast network of corruption which has caused serious decay in Peruvian society.'[16]

In the United States, the collapse of Enron, the sixth company in the world in the Fortune 500, has caused a major tremor after 20 years of relentless progress towards globalisation. Celebrated by analysts, the press and the American establishment as a model company, the firm had only been taxable once in the last five years. Over the same period, it opened 881 subsidiaries in tax havens: 692 in the Caymans, 119 in the Turks and

---

13 cf. *Le Casier judiciare de la République*, Bruno Fay and Laurent Ollivier, Editions Ramsay, 2002.
14 Agence France-Presse, 15th November 2001.
15 ibid.
16 Agence France-Presse, 12th February 2003.

Caicos, 43 in Mauritius and eight in Bermuda.[17] The embezzlement was valued at nearly a billion dollars in six years.[18] Its turnover and profits had been artificially inflated. The management of the firm had hidden the extent of the collapse and had discreetly enriched itself by it. 'Twenty-nine directors and administrators have profited from their knowledge of the real situation of the firm to sell their Enron shares before they were worth nothing. They had sold out for 1.1 billion dollars of securities between October 1998 and November 2001.'[19]

Corruption has been a major scourge in the countries of the former Soviet bloc for ten years now. According to the Director of Public Prosecutions, Vladimir Oustinov, it costs Russia 15 billion dollars a year.[20] In Poland, a recent poll showed that 89% of Poles believed their country to be 'eaten away by corruption'.[21] I have personally noted, in an account given to the OECD, an alarming situation in Bulgaria, where 25% of firms have declared that they have bribed someone in order to close a deal in the public sector.[22] As for Romania, the Prime Minister, Adrian Nastase, has declared the struggle against corruption to be the 'priority of priorities'.[23]

India, Mauritius, Pakistan, Indonesia, Uruguay, Mexico, Nigeria, Angola. I could continue this litany over several chapters. It illustrates the crucial nature of this question at a time when certain European countries are bringing justice to heel, and breaking the thermometer instead of lowering the temperature.

I am convinced that there is a *question of corruption* linked to globalisation, much like the Western democracies had to face up to a *social question* at the end of the 19th century, with the rise of industrialisation.

If that's not a con, what is?

The phenomenon both blinds us and paralyses us. Also, the *question of corruption* has been diluted in the larger and more fluid notion of money

---

17   *Financial Times*, 15th April 2002.
18   *Washington Post*, 22nd May 2002.
19   *Le Monde*, 8th February 2002.
20   Agence France-Presse, 23rd March 2001.
21   Agence France-Presse, 24th January 2003.
22   According to the study by the NGO Coalition 2000, which conducted a five-year investigation into this subject and spoke with thousands of entrepreneurs.
23   Interview in *Libération*, 7th February 2003.

laundering. For, whilst large-scale corruption is a universal taboo (each inquiry causing those in power to bring down the shutters), money laundering is a thriving notion, a much-flaunted obsession of the international authorities.

For fifteen years, conferences, directives, reports and pieces of legislation on money laundering have proliferated.[24] Like all the 'experts', I could spend seven days a week every month of the year across the globe at symposia of every kind dedicated to these questions.

Over time, the term money laundering has come to be a blanket term for the markets of prohibition (drugs, commerce with embargoed countries, or contraband), the parallel economy (prostitution, black market and endemic petty corruption), tax evasion (from an individual defrauder right up to subsidiaries of international conglomerates), false accounting and the corruption of those in power. The word has lost its meaning.

People put the former Nigerian head of state Sani Abacha and his four billion dollars of personal reserves in the same category as the small-time dealer from Birmingham, the raptors, those financial arrangements which allowed the concealment of 504 million dollars worth of losses in Enron's accounts,[25] and the Slovakian prostitute who recycles her money through an Austrian building society.

Treating everything the same way leads to confusion. Money laundering is a distant crime, attributed to offshore financiers, whilst corruption is a more immediate crime, which touches the men and women who lead us.

When the world's experts want to excite public opinion, all they have to do is add up the global drug market and the numbers from the black market, the turnover of counterfeiting, contraband and prostitution. On that scale, the figures are meaningless because the mind is incapable of understanding a given sum beyond several zeroes. How do we make sense of this sort of Monopoly money? When compared with global GDP, one ends up with a range of between 2-5%, half of which represents drug

---

24 The UN Convention against the illicit traffic of narcotics and psychotropic substances, signed in Vienna in 1988, was the first to consider money laundering as a penal infraction – which had to be extended to every country. In 1989, it was followed by the creation of FATF, which made an edict out of the recommendations and published a blacklist of states and territories which did not cooperate.
25 These operations were derisively named after a particularly intelligent and voracious dinosaur featured in *Jurassic Park*.

trafficking.[26] Unfortunately, a Canadian researcher has recently published a study which argues against the numerical assessment of the underground economy. He examined the origin of some peremptory declarations which had been quoted around the world; most of them were just rather fantastical armchair estimates.

Beyond disagreements about numbers, this is the key paradox: despite the international mobilisation and the arsenal of weapons put in place at institutional level, we have drawn a blank. The case of the drug trade is instructive. Simple common sense would lead one to conclude that the results of the struggle are derisory; a few small fry, one or two symbolic hauls a year. 'In 1971, when President Richard Nixon declared the war on drugs, there were just under 500,000 drug-addicts in the United States. At the time, the anti-drug budget was no more than 100 million dollars. Thirty years and a trillion dollars later, the number of American drug-addicts is now estimated at more than five million and the war on drugs is now costing America twenty billion dollars a year on the federal budget alone. If that's not a con job, what is?'[27] writes Michael Levine, a former member of the DEA.

The struggle against the sale of narcotics always runs into a series of obstacles. First of all, political obstacles: most of the great powers have protected criminal circles for geopolitical reasons. After the entry of Soviet troops into Kabul in 1979, the Western and Pakistani secret services recommended that the Afghani mujahadin grow opium to finance their war against the Red Army.[28] In the United States, the official inquiry into the Iran-Contra affair showed that the CIA had collaborated with the Colombian cocaine cartels in order to finance the Nicaraguan Contras. Whilst in Panama, Manuel Noriega, himself paid by the American information services, contributed to the laundering of money from Latin American drug-traffickers. In Europe, independent organisations such as the Geopolitical Observatory of Drugs frequently denounced the tolerance of drug trafficking by the EC authorities. So the major powers are fighting with the left hand that which they are tolerating, possibly even encouraging, with the right hand.

---

26 According to IMF (2002 figures), quoted by Christian Chavagneux in *Rapport du conseil d'analyse économique sur la gouvernance mondiale*.
27 *Black List. Fifteen great American journalists break the law of silence*, Kristina Borjesson, Les Arènes, 2003. Michael Levine is author of the *New York Times* bestseller *Deep Cover*.
28 cf. *Le Monde*, 30th October 2002.

The political obstacles are accompanied by financial ones. Senator Carl Levin's report, published in February 2002 after a year-long inquiry, shows the participation of the largest banks[29] in money laundering, particularly through their preferential treatment of 'correspondent banks'. The economy of prohibition is a source of capital for the financial system, which has adapted itself to receive the profits without getting caught. The banking havens of the Antilles prosper on the traffic from Latin America, and Singapore is getting rich on Burmese drug dollars.

The most respectable establishments are playing a double game. The number one French bank, BNP-Paribas, has branches in eight of the fifteen countries accused by the OECD of not cooperating in the fight against money laundering.[30] Another example of hypocrisy: the number one German bank, Deutsche Bank, has threatened to close its subsidiary in Mauritius, one of the most dubious financial centres on the globe, having been indicted by the service combating the money laundering activities of the Mauritius government, which finally chose to close its eyes to what was going on.

Because of our inability to fully understand the problem, there is a risk of seeing our efforts lost in an absurd black hole. My belief, based on eight years of experience in the area, is that we will not find a solution to the problem of financial crime because it includes too many unknown factors. It is necessary to isolate one variable and concentrate on it. Large-scale corruption is a Gordian knot. If it is cut, our preconceptions will be shaken in a spectacular fashion.

29 He names the Bank of New York, the Bank of America and Citigroup JP Morgan Chase.
30 'Les filiales compromettantes des grandes banques européenes', *L'Expansion*, 28th September 2000.

The Catch

I remember a UN departmental director in his immense double-aspect office overlooking New York, laughing sardonically and saying, 'You have no idea, ma'am. How could you think you'll achieve anything?' This from a man heading one of the departments leading the fight against corruption. Our real enemy is the universal feeling of fatalism that suggests that corruption has always been around, and that questions the usefulness of acting like a latter-day Don Quixote fighting windmills? The fatalists are wrong; everything has changed.

Of course, the marriage of power and money is an old story.

Under the monarchy in 1700, 'to give and make presents' featured as an item in the *Breviary of Politicians* by Cardinal Jules Mazarin. The great ministers were great predators. At the peak of his greatness, Colbert, Louis XIV's finance minister, had managed to amass a fortune equivalent to 5% of the budget of the kingdom: rights to mint coins granted for bribes, factories swallowed up in financial scandals, the bankrupting of the loan reserves, royal bonuses given 'in consideration of service' etc. 'The austere Colbert blithely conflated the coffers of the kingdom with his own. The new factories were an excuse for every sort of trafficking. All the institutions paid him bribes. […] The notion of a State budget was still undefined. It was taken for granted that a minister could also play the role of the country's banker. The difference between a civil servant and employee of the minister was not very clear.'[1]

---

1 'Colbert: le grand serviteur de l'Etat n'a pas oublié de se servir', Pierre-Henri Menthon, *Historia*, October 1996. These excesses were, however, punishable: Certain practices, such as bribery, were categorically forbidden in the 17th century. Several high-profile trials took place, among which were those of the Lord High Treasurer Fouquet in 1661, and the Italian financier Bellinzani in 1680, charged with clandestine payments to Colbert's assistant.

As a result, the Republic which grew out of the Enlightenment was explicitly constructed against *suffrage censitaire*[2] with a property qualification (where the weight of a vote was in proportion to personal fortune), against the jurisdiction of castes (where nobles were judged only by their peers) and against the buying of influence. The revolutionaries reconnected with the Athenian ideal, according to which the 'idiot' was he who thought only of his private interests, whilst a free man worthy of the name would devote himself to the common good; this alone would give meaning to our mortal and incomplete lives. However, democracy's Achilles heel is its vulnerability when faced with individual weaknesses.

Another scale

At the same time, the rise of capitalism has not been without moral dubiousness. The practice of covert commission payments is as old as global commerce. 'Samuel Pepys, First Lord of the British Admiralty (1633-1703), considered that bribes were acceptable as long as they were discreetly slipped under the table [...] Red envelopes in China, *baksheesh* in Arab countries, *matabeesh* in central Africa, *payola* in the Philippines, *propina* in Latin America, the words to designate corruption are innumerable.'[3] The great maritime countries have mostly benefited from piracy, the slave trade and influence-trafficking.

At the beginning of the 19th century, liberals and theorists of capitalism admitted its moral imperfection, hoping that the individual failings and strong points would naturally combine as in the English economist Mandeville's fable of the bees: as in a beehive, the various conflicting forces would end up by working for the common good. Many great fortunes have a shadowy origin. In the USA, at the turn of the 20th century, the 'robber barons', giants of industry and finance, controlled both the economy and the politicians.[4]

For a century, our political history has been punctuated with recurrent political and financial scandals. This could give the false impression that

---

2   Voting system based on ownership of property/tax assessment.
3   'Les jeux dispendieux de la corruption mondiale', Pierre Abramovici, *Le monde diplomatique*, November 2000.
4   cf. Howard Zinn, *Une histoire populaire des Etats-Unis*, editions Agone, 2002.

the affairs with which we are concerned are of the same kind; inevitable but minor accidents, intrinsic to human nature. However, the historical comparison, rather than reassuring us, is worrying. In France, the greatest political and financial scandal of the first five republics, the Panama Canal project, involved about a hundred ministers and parliamentarians. Nicknamed the '*chèquards*', they received secret monies in exchange for voting for a law which would permit the issuing of a large-scale loan to support the project. The sums in play at that time were, in today's money, the equivalent of thirteen million euros, which when compared to the Elf investigation or Angolagate, would represent a mere trifle. The Stavisky affair, money trafficking, the Gaullist financial scandals regarding building contracts; the scandals of times past would barely be considered newsworthy nowadays. The nature and size of corruption facing us has no equal in the history of democracy.

With the financial globalisation of the last 20 years, we have shifted to a whole new dimension. The current large-scale corruption is a radically new phenomenon; it is no longer individual, but systemic. The amounts in question are no longer marginal. On the contrary, the transfer of unearned funds is profoundly undermining our political system.

The emergence of large-scale corruption as a political phenomenon can be traced back to the energy crisis of the 1970s. In 1973, the quadrupling of the price of oil forced the West to find a way of getting back with the left hand the money they were obliged to give to the members of OPEC with the right: arms sales, nuclear installations, large contracts for public works, banking services. The sums in question were such that nothing was going to stand in the way of oil trading.

To give an idea of the level of these transfers, one has only to take a look at the example of the United Arab Emirates – the fourth largest gas and petrol reserve in the world – which has seen its oil revenue multiply by a factor of 25 between 1971 and 1980, whilst the expenditure of the federal state has risen by 70% each year.[5] This windfall was vital for western democracies. The result is enlightening: in the United States, during the energy crisis, the profits of the largest four oil companies rose by 146%.

The era of petrodollars marked the beginning of deregulation of the financial markets at the beginning of the 1980s, which has continued ever

---

5   cf. Roland Marchal, *Dubaï, cite globale*, CNRS editions 2002, p.17.

since. Classic managers and directors clinging to traditional management models were pushed into the background. The intermediaries, lobbyists and financiers struck gold. 'Instead of conducting relationships founded on rules, norms and principles, we now have practices founded on exchange in the widest sense of the term, a universal "trade-off" system,' writes Yves Meny. 'The disposition to corruption is not just a case of an individual's appetite for gain. It is also a reflection of the change in dominant values.'[6]

In keeping with this, the European governments have, since 1977, authorised companies to declare the sums used for corrupt purposes to the taxman as 'exceptional commercial costs'. The expression says it all. These sums are tax-deductible. 'It goes against the general interest and it is immoral. But in a strict sense, you could say that it is in the interest of the company,' explained the spokesman for the proposed law authorising the corruption of foreign civil servants, Monsieur Darne, speaking before the French National Assembly at the time.[7]

On the other hand, in 1977, following the Lockheed Aircraft scandal – the American firm had bribed Dutch, Italian, Japanese and German leaders – the United States adopted the Federal Corrupt Practices Act, which condemns such practices, and which American companies have nonetheless continued to undertake through their subsidiary companies in tax havens.

The use of 'exceptional commercial costs' has been just an opening move. During this transition period, companies, corruptors and the corrupted have understood that they could gain considerable sums at every turn, in all impunity. In France, for example, the state guaranteed these large contracts and their highly remunerated intermediaries against potential default on the part of their clients. All they needed was the so-called 'COFACE consent'.[8] This permission was often decided at the highest level, even during meetings between heads of state. Every kind of underhand behaviour seems to be possible when a decision is made by a powerful figure in complete openness.

---

6   'Corruption, politics and democracy', *Confluences Méditerranée*, no. 15, Summer 1995.
7   This disposition, abrogated by the OECD convention, was introduced into French law in 2000. But it is still technically possible to corrupt foreign civil servants by going through a subsidiary company set up outside the zone covered by the OECD.
8   COFACE is the export insurance company.

During the 1980s and 90s, almost every year, a billion francs' worth of contracts that had not been honoured (for which the commission payments were nonetheless effectively pocketed) were passed in this way through the profit and loss columns of companies' accounts, resulting in a discreet but generous transfer of riches from the public to the private sphere, and confirming the *de facto* blessing given to large-scale corruption. A good part of the sales of conventional arms and nuclear equipment to Iraq before the Gulf War (for a liability of 14 billion francs at the beginning of the embargo[9]) was passed over to French companies by the taxpayer, who had probably, without knowing it, financed several hundreds of millions of francs of covert commission payments along the way![10]

A very narrow pyramid

The sectors where large-scale corruption takes place are restricted, since the most sensitive activities can be counted on the fingers of one hand: energy, public works, armaments, telecommunications, and the exploitation of mineral resources.[11] The strategic advantage is clear: seven out of the fifteen largest global firms are in the energy sector.[12]

In these state-dependent sectors, a few major firms wipe out their competitors and dominate world commerce.

Practices including 'deductions', 'good exchanges', 'retrocommissions' or 'subscriptions' are embedded in the culture. They have been helped along by the globalisation of the financial markets and the multiplication of tax havens, which have gone hand in hand with the liberalisation of finance, like the two sides of the same movement.[13] The global market has facilitated the emergence of global corruption.

---

9 cf. *Notre allié Saddam*, Claude Angeli and Stéphanie Mesnier, Olivier Orban, 1992.

10 Between 1995 and 1999, the average of cancellations was more than 8 thousand million francs, with a peak of 16.5 thousand million francs. In its annual report, the Cour des Comptes (the state body that supervises the financial affairs of public bodies and local authorities and monitors the way public funds are used) noted that 'the operations carried out by COFACE on behalf of the state do not always appear distinctly either in the accounts of the state [...] or in the accounts of COFACE.' And it adds, 'Unlike other discharges of debts, those of the debts managed by COFACE do not figure in the budget of the state or in its accounting.'

11 cf., for example, the 2002 report of Transparency International, which lists these sectors as being subject to generalised corruption in the matter of export contracts.

12 *Fortune* rankings 2002.

13 cf. the study of Ronan Palan, *Tax Havens and the Commercialisation of State Sovereignty in International Organisation*, no. 56, Winter 2002, pp. 153–177.

Large-scale corruption is extremely concentrated, much more so than the legal revenues of the directors of firms registered on the stock exchange, who have, it must be said, already benefited handsomely from globalisation. In fact, the illegal revenues accumulate in the hidden side of power. The Elf case is an accurate reflection of this. It is true that it was mostly those in the upper levels of the hierarchy who had profited from the trafficking since there is a price to be paid for silence. In order not to weigh down the process even more, we had fixed a threshold at which legal proceedings would kick in; they were to begin at one million francs (150,000 euros). Several dozen people thereby found themselves safe from prosecution because their illegal booty – which would have led them, in other circumstances, to any court – was, on the Elf scale, comparable to pickpocketing.

But the pyramid of beneficiaries is particularly narrow at the top: the three principal directors amassed three-quarters of the alleged embezzled funds. Suspicious money transfers represented two and a half billion francs, two billion of which were split between three people. The figures speak for themselves. In a similar fashion, the remainder of the commission payments made to foreign heads of state (who were not included in the case due to diplomatic immunity) was distributed between fewer than ten people. If we extrapolate from the Elf case, we could say that for a country the size of France, large-scale corruption involves no more than one hundred nationals and two to three hundred foreigners.

My international contacts confirm the localised nature of embezzlement. A director of the Asian Development Bank told me how, in order to solve a treasury problem encountered by the state of Kazakhstan, the Kazakh president repatriated in the twinkling of an eye no less than a billion dollars from a foundation based abroad, of whose existence everyone had been ignorant until that moment. In the same way, funds embezzled by President Abacha of Nigeria - four billion dollars – are equivalent to eight times the annual education budget of his country.

The arms example

Another sensitive sector gives us a small but illuminating insight into the extent of the amounts in question. It is well known that a kilogram of armaments is the most expensive product in the world: it combines high technology, ultra-sophisticated materials and the element of scarcity. With

Lagadère, Dassault, Thomson and Giat Industrie, France is one of the biggest global exporters in this area.

During the Elf investigation, several witnesses told how commission payments in this sector reached 20% to 40%. Loïk Le Floch-Prigent explained openly in his book, 'Regarding armament operations, I know that commissions are in the region of 25% at the top end of the market as opposed to 2.5% in the oil world.'[14] A CIA report on Eastern European countries gives a figure of 10%.[15] During a deal passed in 1997 between France and Indonesia concerning armoured vehicles, an official document prepared by the management of Giat Industrie during an industrial tribunal dispute with an employee, fixed the commission at 32%.[16] These figures indicate that margins range from between 10% and 40% of the contract, depending on the sensitivity of the material and the country wishing to acquire it.

This money is officially paid to intermediaries or foreign authorities to support the opening-up of a market. The Elf inquiry showed that a considerable part of these commission payments return afterwards to the firm, either in the bank accounts of senior management, or in an internal secret account. These practices, of which I had already been informed by the chief executive of Ciments Français, have surely not been banished from this corrupt sector which more than any other benefits from protection from defence secrecy.

During the period 1991-1999, the annual – official – arms exports of France rose to 5.61 billion euros (37 billion francs) a year.[17] An average commission rate of 20% would represent an annual 1.2 billion euros in secret funds. A minimum rate of 40% corresponds to 2.24 billion euros (14.7 billion francs) of black market money.[18]

---

14 Loïk Le Floch-Prigent, *Affaire Elf, affaire d'Etat*, interviews with Eric Decouty, Le Cherche-Midi éditeur, 2001, p. 34.

15 These prices are commonly admitted. According to Pierre Abramovici, 'The commissions on arms matters, which in the developed countries are about 5% to 6%, can reach 20% to 30%, sometimes 40%.' (op. cit.)

16 *Le Canard enchaîné*, 26th May 1999.

17 According to the Direction générale à l'armament, which depends on the Ministry of Defence.

18 If one looks for a more precise indicator, it suffices for the same period to concentrate on the four premier clients of France: the United Arab Emirates (63.5 thousand million francs), Saudi Arabia (53.2 thousand million francs), Syria (12.7 thousand million francs), and Pakistan (3.3 thousand million francs). If one applies a rate of 30%, in line with the minimum practice in these four countries, one gets a little more than 6 thousand million euros (39.8 thousand million francs) over nine years, or 675 million euros (4.42 thousand million francs) a year - with just four clients!

In this way, each year in the arms sector alone, between three and four Elf affairs disappear into the Bermuda triangles of the tax havens.

A vital stake

There is no valid reason for thinking that the current governments of the oil-producing and mining countries, or the leadership of the giants of the construction or oil industries, are miraculously unaware of the behaviour that the Elf investigation brought to light. Large-scale corruption is installed in the nerve centres of power. Out of the sixteen largest French companies, eleven are involved in a sensitive sector where large-scale corruption is common: Total, Vivendi Environnement, Bouyges, Vinci, Airbus.[19] But the reality of this is rarely discussed openly. The fact that the greater part of the national media belongs to these groups encourages neither curiosity nor debate. The French television channel TF1 is owned by the Bouyges group, *Le Figaro* and *L'Express* are controlled by the Dassault group, *Europe 1*, *Paris Match* and the majority of the press belong to the Lagardère group.

Nevertheless, fighting large-scale corruption is an essential objective. First of all, in practical terms, keeping watch over a small group of individuals is a great deal easier than seeking to apprehend a mafia circle or an underground economy. But at a deeper level, it is the impunity from which the political and industrial leaders benefit that leads them to protect secret accounts (offshore accounts, financial markets for derivatives, banking havens, international clearing houses sheltered from controls) and allows them to salt away the proceeds of corruption which profits both international traffickers and organised crime. This is the catch.

---

19   Ranking in *L'Expansion* 2002.

Crony Capitalism

'I think you're confusing millions with billions.' The reply was biting, the look scornful and the smile haughty. We were in Vienna on the occasion of the negotiation of the international convention on corruption, and the person with whom I was speaking was not hiding the contempt which any mention of corruption inspired in him. The man was a senior Austrian magistrate. I had just been speaking about the case of the former Nigerian president Sani Abacha, who, by using ghost firms via the big American, Swiss and English banks, had embezzled more than four billion dollars, which had been frozen by the law after his fall from power.[1] He was not feigning incredulity. He just couldn't believe it.

During the Elf investigation, as the results of the international letters rogatory from Switzerland, Liechtenstein and Luxembourg arrived on our desk, retracing the detail of financial movements, we too had had to pass from millions to thousands of millions... The reality of large-scale corruption surpassed our understanding. It was staggering and frightening, too.

Aside from the total sums apparently embezzled over three years, from 1989 to 1993 – more than 300 million euros – we had also discovered the so-called 'subscription' system: a sort of hidden tithe of 40 cents per barrel, which represented more than 150 million euros paid annually to West African leaders. Such sums came close to the annual net profit of a large

---

1   In September 2000, the Swiss banking watchdog implicated in particular, Crédit Suisse and Crédit Agricole Indosuez, as well as the City of London, from which sources came 59% of the money deposited in Geneva by the front companies of the Nigerian dictator (quoted by *Alternatives économiques*, October 2000).

publicly listed company. After his immersion in the phantom accounts of Enron, a director of the Security Exchange Commission (SEC), the watchdog of the American Stock Exchange, spoke of how his world vision had changed: 'If they were able to hide that in such a way over such a short period of time, why haven't other firms done the same?'[2] He had answered his own question.

Two opposing worlds coexist. On the one side, the honourable universe, policed, super-competent, a little condescending of the managing elites; and on the other, crime in its purest expression. It is like a double-bottomed drawer.[3]

Staggering complicity

When an authoritarian regime collapses and the immunity of its leaders is removed, instances of large-scale corruption are brought to light. Between four and ten billion dollars by the Congolese Mobutu Sese Seko; five billion dollars by the Filipino Ferdinand Marcos (two billion dollars of which have been recovered by the government); up to forty billion dollars by the Indonesian Suharto; five to ten billion dollars by Saddam Hussein.[4] Each time this sort of information comes to light, we want to believe that it's a case of individual madness.

But these figures match up with all of the presumed embezzlements in the management of Elf. They tally with the IMF's official studies of Angola, which reveal a discrepancy of a billion dollars a year simply through a comparison of the payments to the state declared by the oil companies and the Angolan public accounts.[5] This figure is a minimum

---

2   *New York Times*, 10th February 2002.
3   The audit report for the Milan public prosecutor's department which analysed the accounts of Fininvest, the holding company of Silvio Berlusconi, shows up this ambivalence. The KPMG auditors had effectively established the existence of a 'Fininvest B' made up of a network of 64 firms whose head offices were in a tax haven, in the British Virgin Isles, in the Bahamas, in Jersey, in Luxembourg… 'They should not show, and should stay apart from the consolidated statement of accounts, in order that the link with the Fininvest group remains secret,' explained the lawyer David Mills, in charge of the financial firm charged with the management of these firms.
4   According to the American journalist Lucy Komisar, 'The Americans are tracking colossal sums, estimated to be several thousand million dollars, taken for personal profit by Saddam Hussein. The tangle of twisted networks, made up by multiple front companies and by secret bank accounts, patiently constructed over the course of years by eminent specialists in Switzerland, Liechtenstein and Panama, is on the point of being unknotted.' (*La lettre du blanchiment*, May 2003).
5   Quoted by *The Economist*, 26th October 2002.

estimation of the embezzlements. The cases of Nigeria's Abacha or Peru's Fujimori, like the confessions made by the former directors of Elf in the criminal court, also give an idea of the scale of the fortunes generated every day by large-scale corruption.

This money is not hidden in some dubious establishment in Nauru or Beirut. For a long time now, large-scale corruption has no longer been a matter of thugs and briefcases of banknotes, like the Japanese 'clandestine quarters' (*ankoku jidai*) where politicians, mafiosi, financiers and senior civil servants seal their agreements. It goes on in the open, in the most respectable financial establishments. It prospers in the City of London and in Zurich. The profits to be gained from it are mouth-watering: according to a commission of inquiry carried out by the American Senate, the yield on the accounts of the beneficiaries of large-scale corruption reaches 25% on average, with peaks of 40%. 'In exchange for these gains, the banks offer their clients guaranteed confidentiality, and a vast range of services to help them manage their fortune, which often include secret agreements, foreign accounts, accounts under a pseudonym and ghost firms. The American banks make fortunes by helping their dubious clients do abroad what is forbidden on US territory. It's a dangerous game. Our banks shouldn't transform themselves into transfer and embezzlement systems for the dirty millions coming from crime and corruption,' writes Carl Levin, the president of the US Senate Commission.[6]

This mechanism is not the exception, but the rule. It also applies to French, American and Spanish large-scale corruption as much as to that in Angola or Mexico. Ever since the petrodollars of the 1970s, financiers have, when it suits them, got into the habit of living above the law and obeying only their own logic. The banking system has put itself at the service of the directors of Elf and those of Enron without the slightest of second thoughts: the same networks, the same offshore arrangements, the same banks. A predatory culture has achieved its introduction to polite society.

There is a double danger. On the one hand, 'indulging' the circles of large-scale corruption 'provokes a feeling of political, intellectual and moral emptiness', explains the Spanish *juez estrella* (star judge) Baltasar

---

6   Conclusion of the session entitled 'Private banks and money laundering', of the permanent sub-commission charged with Senate investigations, 9th November 1999.

Garzón.[7] He equates the image of 'crony capitalism' with that of South Korean capitalism: a closed club of leaders where connivance all too often replaces the law, and where hidden understanding supplants competition, with commissions backing it up.

France also has circles made up of directors of the same caste, where everyone helps themselves as they wish. During a financial inquiry at the beginning of the 1990s, I discovered that several loans for a billion francs, which had not been repaid, had been put into provision by the management of a large bank as if they were an accidental minor loss. The auditor had not written a report; it was as easy as that. However, a family member of the president of the bank had benefited from this magic number.

Large-scale corruption resembles a fissure in a wall which makes the whole building fragile. It's a crack which grows in the dark. It undermines the feeling of belonging that links us to one another. A democracy is a living body; emulation and imitation are normal. To place a client system on top of the social contract makes it unwieldy. That mentality spreads in a concentric fashion. One day, maybe even tomorrow, we shall wake up with the vague feeling of having allowed our communal house to be destroyed.

This connivance between the initiated which disregards nationalities extends, of course, to public affairs. Political and financial solidarities have been changed by globalisation. Thus, for ten years now, the candidates in the American presidential election have benefited from contributions from all over the world, with their share of unsavoury support. 'Foreign firms demonstrate an increasing interest in the American political system [...] All of this blurs the division between internal politics and external commerce. The electors of the American president are global now.'[8]

The Elf inquiry showed a regular interconnection between the secret accounts of the directors of the oil company and the accounts of the rival warlords in Angola and Congo-Brazzaville. The alleged secret account was available to all of them. The Angolagate investigation seems to be covering

---

7   Lecture at Porto Alegro, 2nd February 2002.
8   Roger Cohen, 'Global Forces Batter Politics', *The New York Times*, 17th November 1996. See also the instructive inquiries published on the website of the Center for Public Integrity, in particular the file created in 2002 by Diane Renzulli: 'Capitol Offenders: how private interests govern our states' (www.icri.org). It should also not be forgotten that Pierre Falcone, indicted in Angolagate, had made a gift of 100,000 dollars to the electoral campaign of George W. Bush; a contribution of the same size as that made by Kenneth Lay, the CEO of Enron.

the same ground, revealing astonishingly close links between French celebrities, Russian financiers and African despots.

Once again in the 1990s, during a search, I found a formal contract in the safe of a prominent man in French society. According to the contract, he was acting as 'counsel' – no further detail was given – for the account of a foreign head of state, and was receiving an annual remuneration of three million francs at the time (about 457,000 euros).

I looked up. The beneficiary of this contract looked at me, suddenly a little pale. This document concerned my investigations only indirectly, so I hesitated about whether to confiscate it. Finally, I replaced the contract in its steel box. I felt a barely perceptible sigh of relief all around me. Our host had felt the wind of the bullet; the remuneration represented more than three times his already considerable salary.

From that day, I knew that the great electors of our elites are not always who we think they are.

From 'financial crime' to simply 'crime'

Apart from its political cost in Western countries, large-scale corruption is systematically bleeding the poorest countries to death. The graph below summarizes the situation clearly. It shows, in the 1987-dollar equivalent, the collapse of the GNP per inhabitant of Angola for a period during which the oil revenues of that country have exploded.[9]

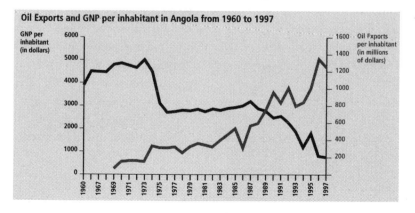

Oil Exports and GNP per inhabitant in Angola from 1960 to 1997

9   cf. Tony Hodges, 'Angola from Afro-Stalinism to petrol-diamond capitalism', Fridtjof Nansen Institute and The International African Institute, 2001. The graph is based on figures from the World Bank.

The difference has lined the pockets of a handful of Angolan potentates and a few dozen important Western businessmen. In Paris alone, 'the Angolan deficit was, in November 1999, 7.4 billion francs, with 2.5 billion of arrears, of which 2.2 billion were covered by the public export guarantee, that is to say, the French taxpayer.'[10] Writing an interim report, the chief of the Brigade Financière spoke of 'colossal profits – at least one billion francs at the current point in our investigations – generated by arms sales to Angola'.[11] In a recent ruling dealing with the renegotiation of the Angolan debt, the Swiss judge Daniel Devaux mentioned the existence of suspect money transfers 'within the framework of a secret organisation working between Geneva, Moscow and Luanda, and pursuing the goal of procuring illicit revenues by criminal means such as corruption and the disloyal management of public interests.'[12] Result: 'Although Angola is potentially one of the richest countries in Africa (with mineral and oil resources), out of 11 million inhabitants, fewer than 50,000 live according to western standards,' states the report of the French Petrol and Ethics parliamentary mission.[13] According to Global Witness, one Angolan child dies every three minutes of malnutrition or of a curable illness.

No lessons have been learned from the Elf inquiry, either in France or abroad. The bridging loans from the large banks continue as if nothing has happened.[14] The subscriptions, the commission and the retrocommission payments still circulate. The heads of oil-producing states and their Western 'dealers' feed their personal accounts in Luxembourg or the Cayman Islands.

However, in removing several billion francs from the secret accounts, the African potentates and the Elf directors have done more than embezzle money: they have created misery. The Cameroonian writer Mongo Beti has written with angry mournfulness: 'Has oil ever been a

10   François-Xavier Verschave, *Noir Silence. Qui arrêtera la Françafrique?*, Les Arènes, 2000, p. 364. See also the report of the NGO Global Witness, 'All the President's Men', which mentions in particular a bank account with 1.1 thousand million dollars in the British Virgin Isles for the use of the Angolan military. The report is available on www.globalwitness.org
11   Report of 9th April 2002 (quoted by *Le Monde*, 23rd April 2003). The inquiry into sales of arms by the firm Brenco to Angola not yet being completed, these figures are only indicative. They could be contradicted, confirmed or augmented before the closure of the investigation.
12   Quoted by *Le Monde*, 24th May 2002.
13   'Pétrole et éthique: une conciliation possible?', 1999, volume 1, p. 149.
14   As far as France is concerned, bridging-loan operations have apparently recently been undertaken in Congo-Brazzaville and in Angola, particularly by Crédit Agricole and Paribas (cf. 'A thousand million dollars of loans secured in a few months', *La Lettre du continent*, 31st March 1999).

source of well-being and progress in Africa? What happens every time is the exact opposite. In my country, we say that oil means the malediction of populations, dictatorship, violence, civil war... In Gabon, there are only broken roads, places to die rather than hospitals, schools which are like kennels... Where does Gabon's oil money go?'[15]

This anger finds a particular echo among Norwegians: more than any other, my native country knows what can be built with mineral resources. Before the first deep-sea explorations in the 1960s, our forebears had an infinitely harder life. The abandonment which Gabon is experiencing should be thought of in these terms. If, for forty years, Gabon had had a transparent and truly democratic regime, that country would have been a model for Africa.

The scandal is taking place right in front of our eyes. Despite a revenue per head worthy of a European country, combining the resources of an African emirate and generous 'development aid' from France,[16] Gabon is one of the African countries where infant mortality has reached record levels.[17] Its neighbour, Congo-Brazzaville, led by Omar Bongo's son, Denis Sassou Nguesso, has been ravaged by several civil wars; to reiterate, both sides were financed by Elf. In 1995, Jacques Chirac turned the French debt of this country (8.4 billion francs) into development aid, still financed by the decidedly accommodating French taxpayers. In parallel, lobbying by Paris brought about the cancellation of 67% of the country's global debt by international authorities. It is, of course, quite unnecessary to point out that, at the same time, the fortune of president Sassou Nguesso went through the roof.[18]

All the same, corruption does not necessarily have to happen. Thirty years ago, Sierra Leone and Botswana, two diamond-producing African countries, had the same GDP. Currently, the former contents itself with 140 dollars per person, whilst the latter managed 3,630 dollars per person. That says it all.

---

15 *L'Autre Afrique*, 1st April 1998.
16 Not to mention the regular cancellations by Paris of Gabon's debt, the most recent (dealing with 400 million francs) having been agreed by Jacques Chirac in 1996.
17 'Life expectancy is only 52 years, only 38% of children are vaccinated against measles – as opposed to an average of 79% in developing countries.' François-Xavier Verschave (according to the United Nations Development Programme report for 1999), op. cit., p. 194.
18 It has been valued at 1.2 thousand million francs before his return to power (*L'Evénement*, 22nd May 1997).

Without handrail or landmarks

In the eyes of history, our generation will bear the responsibility for having let fatal germs develop in the wake of democracy. The spread of corruption is in effect the other side of the coin in a market society where money tends to become the sole criterion to be considered and the only objective for individuals.

By giving encouragement to financial speculation, globalisation has shifted our points of reference. The keystone of this new value system, the salaries of the directors of large firms, has grown exponentially. Our company directors have voted themselves an unreasonable fraction of the added value derived from the firms they lead. We have consented to this uncontrolled increase through a sort of collective amnesia. For example, the allocation to Claude Bébéar, the French CEO of the insurance company AXA, of 1.6 billion francs of stock options in ten years[19] has not raised the slightest objection. The annual general meeting therefore allowed its CEO to amass in broad daylight, and in an entirely legal fashion, that which the directors of Elf had tried to carry off in secret.

Of course, damage to the social contract is not the same thing, but the two behaviours reinforce and legitimise each other. This criticism has been taboo for a long time, but I have decided to start stating it forcefully. During the twenty years when large-scale corruption really started taking off, the boards of directors of firms listed on the stock exchanges – in an obvious symmetry – threw themselves into an overbidding of directors' fees, stock options, salaries, indemnities of every kind... A gradual slide, which, if not exactly criminal, is at least of the criminal variety. The bonuses realised on stock options can reach up to thirty times the total of their salary. You can even take out insurance against a drop in the trading rate! Thirty years ago the ratio between the average and the highest salary of a firm was 1:20. Now it is nearly 1:200.[20]

The stock market depression has not slowed this overheating. The CEO of the Swedish company ABB has been the beneficiary of a guaranteed payment on retirement of 233 million euros: all the while knowing that his firm was deep in the red. In 2001, Lawrence Ellison, the

---

19 *Les Echos*, 28th January 2000.
20 cf. Thomas Piketty and Emmanuel Saez, *Quarterly Journal of Economics*, 2003.

CEO of the computer giant Oracle, renounced his basic salary in a spectacular fashion, which did not prevent him, in the same year, from getting a bonus of 706.1 million dollars thanks to his stock options.[21] The CEO of Alcatel, Serge Tchuruk, who manages a firm in difficulty, which is posting losses and has made redundant tens of thousands of employees, received 900,000 stock options in 2001, then 500,000 in 2002.[22]

This behaviour is morally reprehensible and legally questionable. In fact, according to French jurisprudence, excessive remuneration can give rise to prosecution for misappropriation of public property. But such a strict application of the law threatens small-town bakers in difficulty more than the CEOs of publicly listed firms.[23]

Rather than a means or a lever, power has all too often become either a money-spinner or loot. The mergers of the 1990s realised unequalled profits for company directors and business banks. The gap continues to get wider between the richest 10% and the rest of the population, most of all in the United States, of course, but also in Europe and Asia.[24] Even in Norway, the moral barriers have shifted with disconcerting ease and certain mushrooming fortunes leave the observer baffled.

I have lived long enough not to have many illusions. Put in the same situations, thrown into that orbit of power, most of us would find a thousand reasons to arrogate to ourselves a remuneration which accurately reflected our merits – that is to say, unlimited. Instead of having to assert our legitimacy every morning in the eyes of others, it is easier to invent one's own value system. Our instinct for omnipotence has no limits. When those in power evade the control of society, they reassure each other and become intoxicated by their power. Initiated into the same circles, they succumb to the same drunkenness. It's only human. Large-

21   *The Wall Street Journal*, 18th May 2002.
22   cf. 'Patrons: pendant la crise, les salaires grimpent', *Libération*, 21st May 2003.
23   On 15th October 1998, the criminal chamber of the final Court of Appeal judged that the granting of new salaries and benefits in kind, totalling 4,500 euros per month, to the directors of a firm which was 102,000 euros in the red, constituted an offence of misappropriation of public property, 'because they knew of the very serious financial state of the firm'. See also Cass. Crim. 2nd October 1997, no. 92-83.066 in Eva Joly and Caroline Joly-Baumgartner, *L'Abus de biens sociaux à l'épreuve de la pratique*, Economica, 2002.
24   'In 1999, the *New York Times* established that, in the heart of the most well-off part of the population (20% of households), the increase of the national income had been divided in a profoundly unequal fashion: 1% of households had received 90% of the gains.' Kevin Phillips, *Wealth and Democracy: a Political History of the American Rich*, Broadway Books, 2002 (quoted in translation by Yves Mamou, 'Big Money', *Le Monde*, 3rd December 2002).

scale corruption feeds on what the Italians call the *circolo vizioso dell'arroganza* (the vicious circle of arrogance). It is comparable to hell: it is easy to enter and almost impossible to leave. Impunity allows it to prosper, carefree. And that circle is implacable. As soon as the first bit of resistance gives way, large-scale corruption leads its beneficiaries towards an unreasonable accumulation of money or power. 'Everything yields to its ravages; nothing can stand in its way. Fortune shows its power in the place where no resistance has been prepared, and carries its fury where it knows that there is no obstacle disposed to halt it,' as Machiavelli has it.[25]

But the structures which facilitated Enron's special arrangements or the Elf embezzlements are still there, especially the offshore places and the derivatives, the speculative markets where each operation disappears in ten others. Everything seems to be happening as if, in the great turmoil of globalisation, democracy has lost its landmarks and its way. We have to understand why.

---

25   *The Prince*, chapter XXV.

A Strange Form of Justice

'Great political mistakes almost always come from the fact that men forget that reality shifts, that it is in continual movement. Out of ten political mistakes, there are nine which consist simply of believing to be true that which has ceased to be,'[1] says Bergson. This precept seems to have been written for western democracies. Faced with the deregulation of the financial markets, they have preferred to apply the motto of Prince Salina in Lampedusa's *The Leopard*, 'May everything change so that nothing changes.' They have believed that in maintaining appearances, they can save the essential core behind them.

Yet the financial exchanges are moving more and more outside the sphere of nations. Whilst they were still marginal on the eve of the Second World War, the importance of tax havens has continued to grow. Since the 1960s, the number of offshore subsidiaries of the American banks has increased tenfold. In 1998, after twenty years of financial deregulation, more than a quarter of American investments abroad pass through tax havens.[2]

According to the most recent study, the sum total of assets held in tax havens is almost the size of the GDP of the USA.[3] On paper (for this power is purely virtual), the first economy of the world is comparable with the activity of about 60 pocket-sized territories!

---

1   *La pensée et le mouvant, essai et conférences* (Articles et conférences datant de 1903 à 1923)
2   cf. James R. Hines and Eric M. Rice, 'Fiscal Paradise: Foreign Tax Havens and American Business', *Quarterly Journal of Economics*, no. 109.
3   cf. French parliamentary report on tax havens, quoting Merrill Lynch, which estimates the extent of the assets placed in offshore centres to be 54% of international assets.

One cannot view the world like one did twenty years ago, because it is no longer the same.

These figures represent a legal truth and an economic sleight of hand. The tax havens are just postboxes. The technological revolution of our times means that, with a few clicks of the mouse, via the satellite network, you can make unlimited sums waltz several times a day from an account in Switzerland to an establishment in Liechtenstein from a corresponding bank based in a tax haven, to the trading floor of a venerable establishment in the City of London.

This revolution in the world's commercial habits has taken place in front of our very eyes. The political and legal edifice of western democracies has been imperceptibly modified by it. For the most part, penal litigation falls under the exclusive competence of states. However, since the end of the eighteenth century, the modern democracies have built themselves around the principle of sovereignty; that is to say, the precise opposite of financial deregulation. Even Alfred Jarry's Ubu Roi respected the correct order that reform should take: 'Hurry up please, I wish to make some laws now. I shall reform justice first, then we shall proceed to the finances.' Globalisation has transformed finance, while justice has stayed the same.

Why have we stayed passive in the face of this deep weakness in the democratic system? Because ideas that have taken two centuries to construct, and which we do not yet know how to replace have been largely rendered meaningless by financial globalisation. In sum, we have destroyed without rebuilding; by default, we are leaving old vestigial traces in place for fear of being overcome with vertigo.

The extinction of the enlightenment

To examine the question of large-scale corruption is to raise at the same time the redoubtable question of sovereignty. Voltaire criticised the France of the Ancient Regime, where, on a journey across the country, every time a traveller changed horse, he changed law. The tangle of jurisdictions (royal, seigniorial, ecclesiastic, provosts' courts, bailiwicks[4] and seneschals' courts[5] and so on) was such that judgements could be given five or six

---

4   The office or district of a bailiff.
5   An officer in the house of important nobles in the Middle Ages. In the French administrative system of the Middle Ages, the term sénéchal was also a royal officer in charge of justice and control of the administration in southern provinces.

times over, last a lifetime, or even be transmitted by inheritance. Democracy needs frontiers and protection against the abuse of power. Most of the readers of this book will have been born within clear territorial and legal limits, in a country where the law applies to each citizen in the same fashion, without consideration of title or fortune. This is the inheritance of the Enlightenment.

The right of sovereignty has been a great democratic conquest. The oceans were a place of constant friction until the principle of 'territorial waters' of 12 miles was introduced; then, with hot air balloons and the first aeroplanes, the frontiers were extended skywards – by what is called the Karman line, 62 miles high. Finally, they were extended through the subsoil as far as the centre of the Earth. In this way, physical space became a rigid, multi-dimensional legal and political space, which has been called a 'national cage'. Each cage is contrasted with similar cages which are more and more numerous in line with the proliferation of nations – the number of which has been growing for a century and a half.

Of course, the triumph of the United Nations has included a measure of trompe l'oeil. Since the 1880s, a contradiction has become apparent between the growth of international commerce, which brought about a fluid movement of goods and capital, and the increased sovereignty of states, which added taxes and developed public infrastructure (education, health, transport).

Which legislation should a British ship-owner based in Spain obey? Which state has the right to the taxes on the profits of sister companies which straddle several frontiers? The law has been groping around for answers for a long time. And for good reason: 'Multinational companies do not exist in the eyes of the law,' explains Ronan Palan. 'Strictly speaking, a multinational is not a legal entity, but rather a group of companies spread over the world.'[6] The case of maritime transport, in particular, was a real headache.

To this insoluble problem, which saw sovereignties clashing with each other, tax havens brought a pragmatic response rather than an equitable one.

Of course, the bankers and lawyers immediately rushed in to grab a fiscal advantage from sovereignty conflicts.[7] In the period between the

---

6   op. cit.
7   Notably following a decree from the British House of Lords in 1929, which recognised the fiscal competence of Egypt over a firm based in London, but whose dividends were paid in Cairo (quoted by Sol Piccioto, *International Business Taxation*, Weidenfeld and Nicolson, London).

two World Wars, the Swiss offered the possibility of creating firms protected by Swiss law (and its tax system), whilst their assets were to be found abroad. What ought to have remained a valve, a buffer zone of capitalism, has shown itself to be a windfall for traffickers. The lawyers and financiers of the mafia godfather Meyer Lansky were able in this way to play a determining role in the legal buttoning-up of the Caribbean tax havens.

The trump card of this parallel system, banking confidentiality, has been placed under penal protection. It had been practised by Geneva bankers since the French Revolution, but its reinforcement has been made necessary for the legal blocking-off of fiscal loopholes. In 1932, a French deputy addressing the National Assembly let slip the names of a few of a total of 2000 defrauders, according to a list seized by the police. These people had placed their money in the Banque Commerciale de Bâle to evade tax. 'There were three senators, a dozen generals, and some leading industrialists. […] Straight away, numerous foreign clients panicked. The Banque Commerciale de Bâle had to reimburse large sums. The Discount Bank of Geneva did not survive. […] The Swiss government then put into place in 1934 a new law which placed banking confidentiality under the protection of penal law, an innovation which other territories, such as Beirut, Tangiers, the Bahamas, Liechtenstein and Montevideo copied.'[8]

History, then, legitimizes two practices which have become commonplace. Firstly, the birth of tax havens had nothing to do with excessive fiscal pressure. They appeared almost a century before financial globalisation, at a time when the tax system was moderated; they were, in the first instance, a way of resolving the quarrel over sovereignty. The second practice deals with the penal protection of banking confidentiality, which is often presented, particularly in Switzerland and Luxembourg, as a fundamental liberty associated with human rights, whilst it was above anything else a more effective way of protecting money derived from fraud.[9]

---

8   cf. Christian Chavagneux, 'Secret bancaire: une légende helvétique', *Alternatives économiques*, no. 188, January 2001.
9   'The withdrawal of banking confidentiality constitutes an attack on human rights', declared, for example, Lucien Thiel, the president of the Luxembourg Banks and Bankers Association, taking up the oft-heard refrain. (Quoted in *L'Expansion*, 28th May 1998).

A shameful happiness

Up until 1970, as long as tax havens only concerned a marginal part of capital – particularly personal fortunes – and flags of convenience facilitated certain freight movements, the coherence of our legal system was preserved. The existence of these 'legal interchanges' did not trouble the general equilibrium. During the Cold War, they even allowed secrets and secret operations (financing of guerrillas, arms trafficking, and so on) to be well hidden.

The crisis occurred with the great wave of financial deregulation which, between the years of 1979 to 1984, carried away all the national defences against the circulation of capital. Whilst the principles of transparency and market globalisation were put in pride of place, whilst financial information exploded in volume and technicality, the principles of sovereignty and opacity were deliberately reinforced in the tax havens, the exact opposite of the world as it should be. In Antigua, for example, there has never been any official census of the number of companies placed on the register of commerce.[10]

This is not a natural phenomenon, independent of our will. Almost all of these territories are former British, French, Spanish or Dutch colonies. They developed in our bosom. They are only branches of the exchange centres of London, New York, Tokyo, Frankfurt or Paris, where the heart of finance beats. Such double-dealing is not innocent. It is as if a certain opacity is necessary to guarantee the existence of the shadowy margins that transparency erodes.

Some years ago, New York's district attorney, Robert Morgenthau, denounced this hypocrisy in connection with the Caymans, one of the ten premier financial centres on the planet: 'Opacity is the key word. As far as regulation goes, the place walks off with the medal for laxness. But the Caymans belong to the British crown. Their governor, like their justice minister, is nominated by London. The United Kingdom therefore has the power to put an end to the laissez-faire attitude in its colony, but it does nothing. At the same time, from the financial point of view, the archipelago is an American dependency; most of the offshore banks in the Caymans are in fact managed from Wall Street. Washington, also, could put an end to the offshore schemes. But no one does a thing.'[11]

---

10 cf. Richard H. Blum, *Offshore Haven Banks, Trusts and Companies: The Business of Crime in the Euromarket*, Praeger, New York, 1984.

11 The *New York Times*, 10th October 1998.

It is an embezzlement of the law, a political abuse, for which the generations to come will have to pay the price.

For what is a nation, if not a social contract, a community of citizens who decide to live together? The few citizens of the tax havens of the Isle of Man, of the principality of Monaco, or of the Caymans are not linked by a social contract: in exchange for a few crumbs from the banquet, they make up the *terra incognita* of the world markets, sheltered behind a legal fiction. The Declaration of Independence of the United States, on the 4th July 1776, gave its objective as being 'the pursuit of happiness'... These territories create, with the money of others, a shameful sort of happiness for the benefit of a handful of local leaders.

The law ignores the law

Leaving penal litigation regarding large-scale economic crime in the hands of nation states is perilous, in today's globalized world. With the proliferation of tax havens, the absurd has taken power. First of all, because fiscal inequality is the universal rule today, regardless of the principle of equality before the law. The largest firms are *de facto* outside common law. As soon as your activity is international, playing the system whilst protecting oneself from taxation becomes child's play. We now know that Enron put together in this way eleven 'systems of tax reduction' between 1995 and 2001. These financial and legal arrangements were codenamed after cyclones beginning with the letter 't' (for tax) – Thomas, Teresa, Tammy – or the favourite golf courses of the management of the taxation section – Apache, Renegade, Cochise... Every trick in the book was permitted: raising dividends by placing the sources of profit offshore, accounting the tax reductions as profit after tax, etc. These dodges are alleged to have added up to more than a billion dollars in six years.[12]

A study carried out in October 2000 by the NGO Citizens for Justice of 200 of the largest firms in the world shows that, thanks to the use of subsidiaries in tax havens, 10% of them do not pay a dollar of tax.[13]

Worse yet: large-scale tax evasion has encouraged criminal offshore placements and large-scale corruption. Every inquiry ends up on the

---

12   'Enron's Other Strategy: Taxes', The *Washington Post*, 22nd May 2002.
13   The *New York Times*, (18th February 2002) reported the case of Chevron and Exxon Mobil, which use this technique widely.

blockade of the tax havens. A recent report has shown the legal obstacles that exist in the duchy of Luxembourg alone, 'On average, 200,000 foreign letters rogatory flow into Luxembourg each year, of which a little less than 20% are carried out by investigating magistrates.'[14] When, by chance, an answer reaches the desk of a foreign judge, the information is often unusable. For example, a letter rogatory came back from Luxembourg with the following notes: 'Account in the name of: a client of the bank. Beneficiary of the deposit: another client of the bank.'

If the information is made more precise, purely dilatory proceedings tend to encumber the appeal jurisdictions. Over two years, in 1997 and 1998, only 1.2% of appeals were successful and the rest were rejected. For financial offenders, it is a question of winning time, now as always. As the Luxembourg Banks and Bankers Association blandly puts it, 'the attractiveness of the Luxembourg area will persist for as long as the means allotted to the law are few.'

The political goal of the grand duchy is clear. However, Luxembourg is an 'honourable' country, which takes care of its appearance in order to preserve its status as a founder member of the European Union. Researching judicial cooperation with the Cook Islands, Lebanon or Mauritius would be even more depressing.[15] We have entered into a universe where the law ignores the law, since the rule of sovereignty, pushed to its absurd conclusion, prevents the law from pursuing offences considered most serious in a law-abiding society. We have given birth to a strange form of justice.

A slap in the face of destiny

While the law became ever more powerless against the crimes of the elite, we were continuing to perfect laws which were more and more respectful of human rights.

'A nation's interest in power and riches must give way before the rights of a single man', wrote the Marquis de Condorcet. The last thirty

---

14 Report of Jean-Pierre Zanotto and Edmondo Brutti-Liberati to the Council of Europe, 18th February 2000.

15 Among other examples, there is an edifying monograph devoted to Monaco by the French parliamentary mission on the obstacles to the struggle against money laundering. In this way, the procurator general has the right to rescind requests for banking information 'which damage the sovereignty of the principality'.

years have perfected the protection of the citizen faced with the abuse of power. Norway, in this regard, is a model pupil, almost a naïve one. I have noticed this every day since returning to Oslo. Certain people consider in all good faith that the fact of demanding a penalty fine, as well as the price of the ticket, from an offender who has got onto a train without a permit to travel could constitute an infringement of his human rights! On the grounds of not wishing to issue a double punishment, the Norwegian Supreme Court last summer ruled in favour of a tax fraudster who was appealing against a penal sanction on the grounds that he had returned the money and paid a fine. Tomorrow, will a bank robber have the choice between reimbursing what he has stolen, with interest, or prison? Offences are tending to disappear behind procedural arguments.

I sometimes have the impression that the penal code of my native land was conceived for a country peopled with saints, where phone-tapping is not possible apart from for crimes which would incur a sentence of more than ten years in prison, and where some people believe that the police should use only informers with a clean criminal record.

Norway is a perfect example of where the level of democratic power given to the citizen is directly linked to the strength of the state's laws. This democratic Grail is an ideal type of juridical architecture whereby each citizen benefits from all possible protections with regards to his or her physical and psychological integrity.

No one denies the prosecuting authorities the right to violate the privacy of citizens (their bank accounts, their home, their phone calls, their freedom to come and go) when a crime has been committed.

But no one has yet drawn lessons from the fact that, for a particular category of crimes (such as large-scale corruption, mafia activity or money laundering), the criminals benefit from the unbreakable protection offered by the screen of the banking havens, with their gimcrack sovereignty, preventing the authorities from exercising their elementary prerogatives.

When the holdings in the Channel Islands alone are getting close to the size of half the GDP of Great Britain,[16] the social contract is broken, and the equality of citizens before the law is no longer guaranteed. Worse yet, the individual protection accorded by the legal state gives large-scale

---

16   cf. *Le Monde*, 21st November 1998.

corruption yet further protection to act with impunity. It is a farcical situation.

By an irony of history, one of the two great European jurisdictions, the Court of Justice, sits in Luxembourg! In its decrees on competition, it refers more and more frequently to the protection of fundamental human rights.[17] But the EC judges sit a few hundred metres from 320 financial establishments of the grand duchy, among which is the clearing house Clearstream, an essential part of the dangerous game of derivatives: 50 billion euros exchanged per year; 16,000 accounts opened by establishments from 150 countries, of which 41 are tax havens.[18] The Court of Justice cohabits without compunction with the 12,000 front companies registered in Luxembourg, a haven for financial crime where, in a further irony, the same man performs the functions of the Minister for the Treasury and Minister for Justice.[19]

The new criminal

All European magistrates who have faced up to large-scale financial crime have been subjected to continuous procedural guerrilla warfare by armies of lawyers experienced in the subtleties of increasingly Byzantine procedures. These measures become absurd once the suspect funds cross borders.

In the affair of the Spanish *Guardia Civil* alone,[20] there were 93 appeals before the Swiss courts seeking to prevent the passing of judicial information to Madrid.[21] Towards the end of his fifteen-year term at the head of the public prosecutor's office of Geneva, Bernard Bertossa was spending half his time managing appeals or on time-wasting legal proceedings.

---

17 cf. *Symposium du Luxembourg, Question écrite du Parlement européen*, no. 373, by Lord Kirkhill, and a communiqué from the International Federation of Leagues of Human Rights.
18 A preliminary investigation was opened into Clearstream on 15th May 2001 for 'financial fraud, forgery and use of forgeries, creation of false accounts, failure to declare financial crimes and money laundering.' The 'scenario of systematic manipulation' was, however, set aside by the procureur, Carlos Zeyen in a communiqué which was made public on 9th July 2001.
19 cf. Agefi, 16th September 1998. The Agence France-Presse (18th April 1997) estimates that, given the slimness of resources made available to do the task, a holding company in Luxembourg will be checked out once every sixty years.
20 Luis Roldáán, the head of the Spanish Police had embezzled millions of euros from the force.
21 Lecture by Bernard Bertossa in New Delhi for the OECD, February 2002.

More than twenty appeals resulting from the Elf affair came before the investigating magistrate. The last requests for nullity were only judged after eighteen months. The citizens who listened, day after day, to the transcripts of the hearings of the Elf trial can judge the extent of the alleged embezzlements brought to light by our inquiry. However, the Bar of Paris denounced methods which 'put into question the most fundamental public liberties.' The words 'recusal', 'abuse of authority', 'bias', 'downward spiral' were mentioned almost every day for seven years, by the highest moral, judicial and political authorities in France.

In Italy, the stagnation of the *Mani Pulite* investigation owes a great deal to the increasing difficulties of penal procedures in the area of financial crime. 'Out of the 700 international letters rogatory sent by Italy in ten years to 29 countries, 40% have yet to be answered. It has become almost impossible to prosecute offences for falsifying accounts, due to the brevity of the period before they lapse,' explains Gherardo Colombo, the Milan prosecutor.[22]

Apart from the legal obstacles put in their way, the Italian magistrates have to cope with a violent reaction from the leading elite, in the name of human rights. 'The media have hammered away with the untrue notion that the *Mani Pulite* investigation was a political operation, and not a judicial one. Faced with this bludgeoning, the people have begun to feel doubts about the actions of the anti-corruption magistrates,' says Antonio Di Pietro.[23] The former president of Italy, Francesco Cossiga, had these terrible words for the judiciary: 'The magistrates of the anti-mafia pool are moral, political and judicial torturers.' Silvio Berlusconi has compared *Mani Pulite* to a cancer, and his fellow-travellers denounced the year 1993 as 'the year of the Great Judicial Terror,' a reference to Robespierre. A sign of the times is that the protectors of cross-border crime and grand corruption have reversed roles and words: the movement of the new prime minister is called the 'House of Liberties'.

But who is threatening the social contract? The criminals or those who pursue them? Things cannot go on like this.

In these last few years, the decisions of the European Court of Human Rights give a sad reflection of our society: mafiosi released, drug-traffickers seeking 'fair trial' after the stagnation of their national legal

---

22   Quoted by *L'Hebdo*, 4th April 2002.
23   Quoted by *Libération*, 12th December 2001.

systems which are overburdened and incapable of timeliness... One can easily imagine what will happen when countries widely tainted with mafia activities, from Poland to Turkey, are admitted to the European Union. However, it is correct to say that legally it is not healthy to allow proceedings to spread out over ten or fifteen years, and that a fair trial is a major democratic ideal.

But practically speaking, it is not possible to justify leaving the current impunity any longer: it benefits the mafiosi and those involved in large-scale corruption. Nor is it possible to stand idly by while the spirit of our laws is embezzled by the artificial sovereignty of a few territories which draw their prosperity from crime and fraud.

There are two possible solutions which are being tested to different degrees in Italy and France. Firstly, the legal system is reworked; new laws favourable to large-scale corruption are introduced, legal cooperation between states is prevented, and the die is cast. The legislator makes the traces of the crime disappear through sleight of hand instead of fighting it himself. Gherardo Colombo thus estimates that, by its retroactive effect, the new law on falsifying accounts will invalidate half of the *Mani Pulite* proceedings, due to the reduction in time before the crime lapses. One can of course legitimise tax fraud and complicate to the extreme the procedure for mutual penal aid.[24] But democracy would then only be a façade.

Is this the world we want to live in?

The second solution is to invent a new political and judicial approach to those crimes which pay no heed to borders. The extent of financial crime is a political challenge. A financial criminal is nothing like those 'criminal types' that 19th-century criminologists sought to define. He doesn't have a sinister appearance and a scarred cheek; he is a respectable man in a dark suit, handmade shoes, slimline watch and decorations on his lapel. He inhabits two worlds, which in his mind never meet. His personal actions are not a matter for the common world. He feels himself to be above the law because he can buy it, bypass it, or violate it.

It is up to us to rise to the challenge set by the modern financial criminal.

---

24 'If even a tiny stamp is missing on one of the transmitted documents – files can sometimes run to several thousand pages – the defenders of the accused can request that the file be invalidated. In the same way, in order to be accepted in Italy, the seizing of a document abroad must be done through a process identical to that set out in the Italian penal code, or else it will be rejected. A real headache for the Swiss confederation.' (*Le Temps*, 4th October 2001.)

Hope

For twenty years, as a magistrate, I have had to keep silent. From now on, my only power is speech. In this book, I tell the tale of the world I have discovered; I try to give meaning to a string of scandals which defy common sense. This, in itself, is already something. For the way we look at the world builds our sense of identity. It allows us to go forward on firm ground. Emile Durkheim wrote, 'The set of common beliefs and feelings of a society forms a system which has its own life; one could call it the collective conscience.'[1] These pages deal with our collective conscience.

The quotations at the beginning of this book are intended to show that I have placed it under the patronage of the historian Marc Bloch, whose on-the-spot recounting of the 'strange defeat' of 1940, gave meaning through its lucidity, to his engagement in the Resistance. Also under the tutelary protection of Primo Levi, whose work remained underground for fifteen years, because one often has to wait alone, going against the current, until minds are ready to hear the truth. A true word, even if it is upsetting because it breaks a taboo, can, in its way, put the world on the right track again.

Financial globalisation and the technological revolution have profoundly shifted our points of reference. Without limits, without rules, in silence, large-scale corruption has spread, risking the implosion of our democracies and the destruction of public confidence, that indispensable ingredient in all political action. Because a whole world has disappeared, taking with it a collection of values, practices and references which no

---

1   *The Division of Labour in Society*, book 1, chapter 2.1.

longer coincide with reality, we believed that the notions of justice and injustice no longer made sense. And that they have been replaced by the only universal value: money.

We were wrong. Nothing disappears from the collective conscience: everything merely transforms itself. At the end of the 18th century, the philosophers of the Enlightenment sought to translate their concept of society into criminal law. They established a new balance of crimes and punishments, banishing torture and the death penalty, and protecting the individual against the abuse of power. The great transformation of the economic and global equilibrium should encourage us in turn to invent a new order of crimes and punishments, which would remedy the impunity of the powerful and re-establish the equilibrium of justice.

The creation of the International Criminal Court has been a first step. The struggle against large-scale corruption will be a second. For the former and the latter, it will probably take a generation to reverse the course of matters. But the method of reversal is there. Unquestionably.

To crystallise the international movement struggling against large-scale corruption, I wanted to collect into a simple text, comprehensible to all, a series of essential measures designed to weaken impunity. They are of little cost to the community – especially when compared to the injustices that they are seeking to rectify. I asked men and women whom I admired to engage themselves openly and to help me get this text, the *Declaration of Paris*, off the ground.

The strongest response I have encountered comes from the men and women who have fought for freedom, like the family of Aung San Suu Kyi,[2] Pius Njawe[3] and Wole Soyinka[4] and from those who know the

---

2   A non-violent pro-democracy activist and leader of the National League for Democracy in Myanmar (Burma), and a noted prisoner of conscience. Awarded the Nobel Peace Prize in 1991, she is currently under house arrest. An intermediary was supposed to present the text of the *Declaration of Paris* to Aung San Suu Kyi at the beginning of June 2003. I was attaching great value to the possible signature of this universal symbol of the fight for human rights, who has often protested against the corruption of power and denounced the pressure brought to bear on the regime by the big international firms, including the French oil company Total. Symbolically, the launch of the *Declaration of Paris* was dedicated to her.

3   Editor-in-chief of the independent newspaper *Le Messager*, he is Cameroon's most beleaguered journalist and one of Africa's most courageous fighters for press freedom. Since 1990, he has been arrested more than 30 times and has faced legal action on charges ranging from defaming the head state to publishing false information. *Le Messager* has been censored and closed down, its office equipment confiscated and its staff arrested, fined or tortured in an effort by President Paul Biya to silence the critical voice of the country's few independent papers.

moral and political cost of large-scale corruption, such as Salviero Borelli, David M. Crane and Bernard Bertossa. This has not surprised me. Resisting the abuse of power and preventing the powerful from escaping the law are two sides of the same fight for human dignity. Only the inversion of values, which happens in times of change, could have let people think that the struggle against corruption threatened the rights of man.

The Declaration of Paris is a milestone. It sets out three simple principles for the reconstruction of just justice.

Transparency is the corollary of freedom:
Transparency without freedom is an infringement of human rights. Freedom coupled with opacity is an open door for crime.

Judicial globalisation is indispensable to economic globalisation:
The countries which protect the proceeds of crime or fraud must be excluded from the game and refused banking privileges.

The crime of the powerful is damaging to the higher interests of the nation:
Increasing penalties, introducing civil confiscation[5] and banking vigilance are the instruments for preventing and cracking down on this threat to society.

Today these ideas are considered unimportant, and because of that, they are all the more precious in my eyes. For sometimes a very little thing, a simple event, is enough to change the order of things which seemed immutable.

One of the most astonishing meetings I have been privileged to have since my return to Norway was probably that with Kristian Ottosen, one of the last survivors of Struthof.[6]

---

4   Nigerian writer, poet and playwright awarded the Nobel Prize in Literature in 1986. He has been an outspoken critic of many Nigerian administrations, and of political tyrannies worldwide, including the Mugabe regime in Zimbabwe. During Abacha's dictatorship, Soyinka left the country on voluntary exile and has since been living abroad. When civilian rule returned in 1999, he accepted an emeritus post at the university on the condition that they bar all former military officers from the position of chancellor.
5   This principle exists in Ireland, *Proceeds of Crime Act 1996* and in the United Kingdom, *Proceeds of Crime Act 2002*. It offers courts the possibility of confiscating, without penal proceedings, goods of which the owner cannot give an account of acquisition by legitimate resources.
6   Natzweiler-Struthof in Alsace was the only concentration camp established by the Nazis on French territory.

I had been fascinated by his story. First of all, because when one is advocating an increased suppression of large-scale corruption and stronger means to prosecute the crimes of the elite, it is always a good thing to remember the ravages of another system: that of incarnating evil in the Jews and seeking to eliminate it. Nazism imposed an all-powerful state and created a hell on earth. In struggling against large-scale corruption, we are not seeking to destroy intrinsically evil people, but rather to re-establish the balance between the weak and the strong.

But beyond that, the actions of this man are fascinating. Deported to the camp at Sachsenhausen, he spoke German, which allowed him to get a protected job at the post office in the camp. He could have curled up into himself and waited for the end of the nightmare and made the most of his fate – enviable compared with that of his fellow prisoners. But he had a very simple idea. The Norwegian authorities sent parcels to the deportees. Many arrived wrongly addressed. The 'Nacht und Nebel'[7] operation was devised precisely so that deportees disappeared without trace. So, with just a pencil and a stolen sheet of paper, Kristian Ottosen decided to carry out an inquiry; he quite simply questioned the deportees who arrived from other camps about so-and-so whose letter had been wrongly forwarded to that address, to find out where they were being held. In this way, he discovered the existence of an invisible camp, not listed: Struthof, where he would subsequently be deported himself.

One by one, for months, he drew up a list of thousands of Norwegian deportees with their exact place of detention. Then he got the document out of the camp by giving it to a heroic young Norwegian woman, Wanda Heger, who was allowed to enter and leave the camp each week. The list, with the mediation of the Swedish Red Cross, led to the operation of the thirty 'white buses' which crossed Germany, going from camp to camp to free all the Scandinavian deportees.

I see this as a demonstration of the potential that we all have, each in our own way, to render the world a little better. If this man worked this miracle in the worst of worlds, why can we not act in our free world?

Often, my friends despair of the tales I tell. It is possible that these pages will frighten them all the more. They would then be drawing the

---

7   'Night and Fog'. A directive of Adolf Hitler on December 7th, 1941, resulting in the disappearance of many political activists throughout Nazi Germany's occupied territories.

wrong lesson from my story. Even though it is about crime from the first to the last page, it is also a book about hope. To reprove others is not an ideal for anyone, and the figure of the lawgiver inspires in us a legitimate distrust. As Pascal has it, 'he who seeks to be an angel ends up a devil.' On a personal note, I've been misrepresented as a result of struggling with, constraining, arresting, prosecuting, imprisoning or bringing to court men and women. The image of the Iron Lady is probably the furthest possible from the real me; it does not reflect my nature but the toughness of the circumstances. In life, I like nothing better than to give to others and to receive love. Like Candide, my ideal would be to cultivate my garden.

Events have taken a different turn. Even though the exercise of authority was internally painful to me, I am proud of having taken it on. For it is an indispensable function of life in society. Seeing justice done is a form of creation, which soothes suffering and prevents avoidable misfortunes. Penal sanction is like the lighthouses along the coasts: it guides us. And sometimes, it enlightens us.

I am writing the last pages of this book in the midst of a great explosion of nature. On 26th September 2002, I could still swim in the Oslo fjord, in warm seawater and temperatures of more than 20°. A fortnight later, the snow came. It stayed until April on the hill where I live. I went abroad for a week, and on my return the buds had appeared. No one enjoys the light as much as those who are deprived of it for six months. 'The winter's night in the open' which I have lived through over the course of these years of combat and threats will not have been in vain. I probably relish the savour of this brightly-coloured spring all the more. But, above all, I want to testify before everybody that a future is possible.

Paris and Oslo, August 2002–May 2003.

The Declaration of Paris
A Call for Action Against Large-scale Corruption

We, citizens from around the world, drawn from the four corners of the Earth and from countries rich and poor, come together united in our determination to denounce in the strongest terms the devastating impact of high-level corruption and the levels of impunity that facilitate it, and to demand concerted national and international measures to combat it. We unequivocally condemn all those whose actions and whose inactions have contributed to the crisis of corruption now sweeping the globe, deepening poverty; undermining emerging, and even developed, democracies; and eroding fundamental human rights in many societies. And as we condemn them we unite in a call for urgent action.

The opening up of markets has brought an explosion of corrupt practices. 'Levies', 'commissions', 'kick-backs' are commonplace. They frequently involve people in high positions in government and major international corporations. The perpetrators of these crimes are all too ably assisted by the banking institutions of offshore havens and by bank secrecy laws. But most of all they are protected by systems of impunity that place the leading figures involved beyond the reach of the Rule of Law. Even where the criminals are not formally immune from investigation and prosecution, the officials and the private sector operators are protected in practice by slow and unreliable systems for the taking of evidence across international boundaries. This state of affairs cannot be permitted to continue.

The most abused business sectors are well known: major construction works, the defence industry, aviation, oil, gas and mining. A relatively small number of large corporations, sheltering behind the protection afforded them by their own governments no less than those of the countries they are dealing with, rig public procurement contracts. As a consequence, many people around the world are forced to pay too much for far too little, and are left to meet the debts their corrupt rulers and their corporate conspirators leave behind.

In the process vast fortunes have been amassed – fortunes based on activities that are deepening poverty and denying development to millions, and fortunes more often than not invested in safe havens in Europe and North America.

We believe that rules can and must be developed to meet the challenges of a changing world. The United Nations Convention Against Corruption, presently being prepared in Vienna, has reached a critical stage in its negotiations. It can and it must serve as a radical agent of change. There is scope, too, for the Financial Action Task Force on money laundering to play a much more forceful role in developing its recommendations. We appeal to all those involved in efforts to reform international arrangements to rise to the challenge and act together in anticipating future developments so that large-scale corruption can be fought and defeated.

We therefore declare our convictions that the following steps must be among those that are taken and that they be incorporated, as appropriate, into the new United Nations Convention Against Corruption and the FATF Recommendations:

1. *To make investigations more effective and no less fair:*
   States must review their laws and ensure that no form of executive, parliamentary, diplomatic and judicial immunity can be used to obstruct financial investigations (with committal for trial being subject to a vote of the House concerned only if this is a constitutional imperative);

   States must review their practices and procedures so as to ensure that these cannot be abused in order to obstruct investigations by delaying the transmission of evidence to foreign courts;

   States must ensure that their laws do not contain limitation periods which facilitate trials being terminated prematurely for no other reason than the fact that a defendant has successfully delayed the trial from concluding on time;

Banks must be forbidden from opening subsidiaries or transaction business with establishments in any countries or territories, which are failing to play their full part in international judicial cooperation;

Banks and financial institutions must be required to record and retain records of all interbank transactions, including a complete identification of all beneficiaries and those who order the transfers;

Professional privilege as between lawyers and their criminal clients must be lifted where there are serious grounds for believing that lawyers have been involved in assisting criminals to launder their ill-gotten gains.

2. To ensure that offenders do not benefit from impunity, but are convicted:

States must ensure that officials in positions of power who are in possession of inexplicable wealth are required by law to provide a credible explanation for their wealth and provide for confiscation of assets should they fail to give a reasonable explanation to the satisfaction of a court;

The penalties for serious corruption should reflect the grave damage the offences do to the state and its citizens.

3. In order to deter these serious forms of corruption:

Listed corporations must be compelled to declare in their consolidated accounts, on a country-by-country basis, the net revenues (taxes, royalties, fees, bonuses, revenue shares, etc.) paid to the governments and state owned corporations of all countries in which they operate (whether inside or outside the country), so as to ensure transparency of transfers between corporations and states;

Judicial competence must be conferred on the jurisdiction where an international corporation has its principal office, so that prosecutions can take place when its subsidiaries are accused of corruption and the state where the offence was committed does not have the ability or the will to pursue the case;

Banks must be required to maintain enhanced watch and to report suspicious transactions where they hold accounts for persons who are at risk of being involved in serious corruption such as politicians, senior officials and leading private sector persons who are operating in 'high risk' business sectors.

Breaking down the ramparts of serious corruption is an urgent necessity if development processes are to be unlocked for the benefit of all and to build a more peaceful and secure world. Our own generations must do what we can to restore confidence in our political and economic systems and those who hold positions of leadership within them. In an era of globalisation, those who lead us bear immense responsibilities. To give the rest of us hope, they must be above suspicion and they must take the steps we have outlined as a matter of highest urgency.

If you wish to sign the Declaration of Paris you may photocopy and sign the preceding pages and send them with your address to:
Les Arènes
Déclaration de Paris
33 rue Linné
75005 Paris
France